My Adventures as a Psychic Nurse & Medium

Spirits Everywhere!

SHIRLEY SMOLKO, RN, BSN, MBA, MSA

Joe Smolko, M.Ed., Editor

Cavallaro Publishing

Copyright © 2021 by Shirley Smolko

All rights reserved. No part of this book may be reproduced in any manner whatsoever without written permission except in the case of brief quotations embodied in critical articles and reviews.

ISBN: 978-1-7345146-6-7 (Paperback)
ISBN: 978-1-7345146-7-4 (E-book)

Cover design by Shirley Smolko

Second Printing 2023

First Printing, 2021

Library of Congress Control Number: 2021901967

This Completely Revised Edition was Previously published as *Adventures of a Psychic Nurse: Spirits Everywhere!*

DISCLAIMER

This book is narrative nonfiction and should be considered a literary work. It reflects my present recollections of experiences over time. Events have been compressed, and all dialogue has been recreated to represent what may have been said. Therefore, the dialogue in this memoir should be considered representative dialogue. I have tried to recreate events, locales, and conversations from my memories of them. To maintain their anonymity in some instances, I have changed the names of individuals and places. I may have changed some identifying characteristics and details such as physical properties, occupations, and places of residence.

Shirley Ann Smolko and Cavallaro Publishing have no responsibility for the persistence or accuracy of URLs for external or third-party Internet Websites referred to in this publication and does not guarantee that any content on such Websites is, or will remain, accurate or appropriate.

Designations used by companies to distinguish their products are often claimed as trademarks. All brand names and product names used in this book or on its cover are trademarks of their respective owners. The publishers and the author are not associated with any product or vendor mentioned in this book. None of the companies referenced within the book have endorsed the book.

I dedicate this book to my wonderful husband and Editor, Joe. There was a time early in our relationship, before we were married, when he told me he believed that when you're dead, you're dead. He's changed his mind!

CONTENTS

DISCLAIMER - v
DEDICATION - vii
PREFACE - xi

~ one ~
Growing Up With The Dead
1

~ two ~
Spirits Invade My Dreams
16

~ three ~
Spirits In The Astral
37

~ four ~
Spirits On The Job
46

~ five ~
Hospital Haunts
65

~ six ~
Dining Out With The Spirits
78

~ seven ~
The Spirits Are Always Out & About
93

~ eight ~
On Vacation With The Spirits Of Italy
112

~ nine ~
Spirits Of Relatives Who Said Goodbye
137

~ ten ~
Spirits In My Reading Room
149

~ eleven ~
My Scariest Ghost Investigations
162

EPILOGUE - 199
ABOUT THE AUTHOR - 202
OTHER BOOKS BY THE AUTHOR I - 203
OTHER BOOKS BY THE AUTHOR II - 205

PREFACE

The few who dared to step through the door, after giving it a final push, have found the powerful consensus that we can lead a life independent of the physical body and, by implication, a life that continues after death.
~ Ziewe, Jurgen.Vistas of Infinity: How To Enjoy Life When You Are Dead." Jurgen Ziewe, 2015, p. 10.

It probably comes as no surprise to you that hospitals are haunted. I should know—I am a psychic medium who happens to be a nurse and has worked in many old and very haunted hospitals. Haunted hospitals, however, aren't the only places where you'll find spirits. They are everywhere, all around us. They can be found in all types of public places, such as work, restaurants, massage parlors, grocery stores, churches, museums, beauty shops, government agencies, and the list goes on. Wherever you find people, you'll find spirits. It's been my experience that spirits haunt people more often than they haunt places. That's why you can find them everywhere you go.

Allan Kardec, the nineteenth-century founder of Spiritism and author of five books known as the Spiritist

Codification, apparently thinks so too. In *The Spirits' Book II* (1857), he writes:

> *Spirits are everywhere. The infinite reaches of space are filled with them in infinite numbers. Usually imperceptible to us, they are constantly beside us, observing and influencing us. Spirits do not occupy a circumscribed space. They are everywhere and are perceived by and regularly associated with human beings. They constitute an invisible but active society that constantly interacts with our own. Spirits constantly exert an influence on both the physical and mental environments of the Earth. They constitute one of the powers of nature since they can act equally upon matter and thought. They are the cause of many sorts of previously unexplained or misinterpreted phenomena, which now find a compelling rationale in the Spiritist Doctrine.*

He writes in an issue of the *Spiritist Review, Journal of Psychological Studies (1878)*:

> *We are incessantly surrounded by a cloud of spirits that occupy the space around us, despite the fact that we cannot see them, watching our acts and reading our thoughts, some to do us good, others to do us harm, whether good or bad spirits, accordingly.*

The spirits have told me their invisible world is as real and solid to them as our physical world is to us. It interpenetrates and extends around the earth and is made of etheric energy, which vibrates at frequencies beyond the physical spectrum.

In the book *Heaven and Hell* (1758), the eighteenth-century Christian mystic, theologian, scientist, and philosopher Emanuel Swedenborg states that the spirit world exists alongside our physical world. He describes creation as being made up of two separate but coexisting *worlds*: the physical world and the spiritual world. The physical world includes everything you see around you—landscapes, other people, your own body, etc. In the spiritual world, people have bodies, live in houses, enjoy community life, and are surrounded by landscapes like those on Earth. However, things work very differently in spiritual reality. Everything there is vivid and much more alive. What dead people see depends on what they are thinking. Spirits are only as near or as far away as our thoughts of them. Their thoughts of us can bring them to us. Our thoughts about them can also bring them to us. The spiritual world consists of unseen realities that we do not fully encounter until after death: heaven, hell, and the world of spirits in between.

If the spirits want to, they can watch everything we do. They watch us in the same way we watch television. You know you can tune in and watch your favorite TV show anytime, but do you want to spend every moment watching TV? Probably not, and neither do spirits. Your loved ones in spirit are not watching you to judge you. They simply want to give you the love and support you need on your path. They are totally aware of those times when you need privacy and will turn away from observing certain situations if you ask them. In the physical realm, when a door is shut, we respect it and know that the person behind it needs privacy. It works the same way in the spiritual realm. To your loved ones in spirit, what you do in the bathroom is usually not of interest to them. It's the special occasions, milestones, and celebrations that your loved ones in spirit want to see. This is also true for those times in your life when you're experiencing struggles or a crisis; they will often stay with you to give you protection, support, and guidance.

Spirits have access to universal information contained in the Akashic Record, also known as the Book of Life. The Akashic Record is a non-physical compendium of the history of the universe that is imprinted on the Akasha. It includes all the thoughts and actions of every person throughout time. Spirits can use this record to gather all of the details surrounding the issues in your life so they can offer insight. In Hinduism, Akasha refers to space and is believed to be the basis and essence of all things in the material world. It is the first material element created from the astral world; the other four elements are earth, air, water, and fire. It is also the stuff of which gods, celestial beings, and souls are made. There is one caveat to getting guidance or insight from spirits: never allow a spirit to tell you how to live your life. Spirits that are coming from a good place will honor your free will and not try to control you.

What the spirits have told me over the years about their world is that it looks a lot like the physical world, only more beautiful, which is basically what Emanuel

Swedenborg suggested in his book *Heaven and Hell.* Most of the spirits I have channeled told me they were in heaven. I have never communicated with a spirit that told me it was in hell, but that doesn't mean that such a realm doesn't exist. Everyone I have read about who had a loved one who committed suicide told me they believed their loved one was probably in hell. Contrary to popular belief, I have never had a spirit who died from suicide tell me they were in hell. They have always told me to tell their loved ones that they are at peace and in a good place. On the other hand, I have communicated with many spirits in the middle astral realm (the spiritual realm closest to the material world) who said they were afraid to move into the Light because they feared that they would be sent to hell. Regardless of a soul's abode, whether they are in heaven or hell, I've been told by the spirits that their world coexists and intermingles with ours. Spirits are all around us. Spirits are everywhere!

~ One ~

GROWING UP WITH THE DEAD

[Let] nothing but good be said of the dead.
—Chilon (6th century B.C.) One of the Seven
Sages of Greece

My Story

My first memory of interacting with Spirit occurred when I was five years old. My Grandma Nora had a picture of her parents hanging on the wall of her living room. I recall pointing to that picture and telling my grandma, "I sat on Papa's lap on the big porch," to which my grandma replied, "No, Honey, you couldn't have. You didn't sit on Papa Joe's lap because he died about five years before you were born." I remember arguing with my grandma and saying, "Oh yes, I did sit on Papa's lap!"

Hoping to convince my grandma, I described in detail my great-grandparents' huge front porch with the big bay window. My grandma said, "Yes, Honey, they did have a big porch with two bay windows, one on each side of the front door." She became silent and didn't say another word after that.

I saw my first aura when I was seven years old while attending church with my Grandma Nora. I sat quietly on the pew beside her while I colored the lesson I received in Sunday School earlier that morning. The increased tone and volume of the minister's voice captured my attention, and when I looked up at him, I noticed the colors purple, red, blue, and yellow swirling around his head and shoulders. In a whisper, I asked my grandma if she saw all of the colors around Pastor Nowell. She placed her index finger over her mouth and shushed me, saying, "We'll make an appointment to have your eyes checked soon." I was basically told that something was wrong with my eyes. So, from then on, every time I saw an aura, I told myself it was just an eye problem. I actually had to wear prescription glasses a few years later. I guess her suggestion that I needed an eye exam was some kind of self-fulfilling prophecy.

Not until I was a young adult did I discover that what I had actually been seeing all those years were auras. I eventually learned that the colors of an aura have meaning. Once I learned those meanings, I understood that the colors I had seen swirling around Pastor Nowell's head and shoulders represented his emotional and mental state. Purple represented divinity—he was talking about

God. Red reflected his passion for what he was saying about God. Medium blue indicated his determination to communicate his message to the congregation, and yellow represented his thoughts about what he was saying. Taken together, these colors told a story about Pastor Nowell's state of being. Once I embraced the belief that seeing auras was normal and not some kind of eye problem, I began to see them more frequently around people and animals. I even discovered that not only are there colored auras, but there are clear ones as well.

In my experience, clear auras appear as a clear gas rising up and swirling around an individual's head and shoulders. The best way to describe a clear aura is that it looks like heat rising from hot, wet pavement. The first time I saw this kind of aura, I remember asking Spirit what it meant. The answer I received was that clear auras envelop people who practice magical arts and are highly attuned to creative energy. This creative energy has been known by different names in different cultures. It has been called Chi, Ki, Prana, Mana, Deeksha, Kundalini, Shekinah, and the Holy Spirit. Whatever you choose to call this energy, it is the spiritual substance and power that allow us to create our realities as we will them to be. Spirit went on to tell me that we can direct this force with our thoughts, beliefs, and focus to create what we desire in life. Magical individuals who use this spiritual substance are always surrounded by a clear, vaporous-looking aura. This spiritual substance is always waiting to respond immediately to their beck and call.

For as long as I can remember, I have had vivid dreams

that I always recall upon awakening. I have both precognitive and retrocognitive dreams. Many precognitive dreams I have experienced over the years were warnings about events to come, either for myself, loved ones, or friends. Some of the time, the warnings were balanced with the assurance that things would be okay in the end. For example, I dreamed I would have a car accident in the snow three days later and not be injured. In the dream, my car rolled several times, and when it came to a stop, I was pulled out through the sunroof by a big hand, which I perceived as representing the hand of God or divine intervention. In addition to the hand coming through the sunroof, I heard a booming male voice say, "Be still and know that I am God." Three days later, my prophetic dream became a reality—I had a car accident in the snow. It wasn't snowing when I left home. Had it been snowing, I would have never left the house because of the warning I received.

When I was in my early twenties, I had a dream about a friend of mine who was seven months pregnant with her second child. In the dream, she lost her baby due to placenta previa, a condition where the placenta lies low in the uterus and partially or completely covers the cervix. The placenta may separate from the uterine wall as the cervix begins to open during labor. I was troubled by the dream, so I called my friend the next day to see how she was doing. I didn't tell her about the dream. I just encouraged her to take care of herself and to call the doctor immediately if she experienced anything out of the ordinary, like bleeding. I was in nursing school at that time, so I used that as an excuse for conveying the information because I didn't want to alarm her. A couple of days later, she went into labor and lost the baby. She also came close to losing her own life. When I visited her in the hospital, she asked me why I had said what I did when I had talked to her on the phone earlier that week. I confessed that I had a dream about her losing her baby, but I didn't want to scare her. A good portion of my precognitive dreams have been about relatives, friends, or co-workers who will die soon. I will talk about some of those dreams later in the book.

Not all of my dreams about the future have been warnings. Some have been about good things to come, such as the birth of my daughter. I had a prophetic dream in which I received details about what she would look like when she was born, such as her eye and hair color, gender, weight, and length. She was born with the exact traits of which I had dreamed: black hair and brown eyes, seven pounds and three ounces, and twenty-one inches long. I have also had dreams that prophesied the person that some of my relatives would marry. At the time of the dream, some of these individuals would not even be involved with the person they would eventually marry. For example, I dreamed that my first cousin, Mandy, came to me wearing her wedding gown and said that she would be getting married soon. She also said she wouldn't be changing her last name because she didn't need to. I didn't understand exactly what she meant by her comment until I met her fiancé. Although they were definitely not related, Mandy and her fiancé had the same last names.

Most of my retro-cognitive dreams have occurred as a result of spirits that have come to me to tell their story. I have been able to validate many of these retro-cognitive dreams from spirits through historical records such as the census, newspaper articles, and books. I feel that these spirits were looking for absolution through confession. Telling me their story allowed them to purge themselves of guilt and obtain the forgiveness they believed they needed so that they could cross over. These are the souls stuck in the astral realm because they are afraid they may go to hell or purgatory if they cross over into the light. As any good medium would do, I allowed them to vent their concerns about what they believed might lay ahead of them if they crossed over.

To help them overcome their fears and heal their spiritual bodies, I tell them there is forgiveness for everybody because there is a law of grace given to us by the Creator whereby we may forgive ourselves and others for any harm we have caused or others may have caused us. Most importantly, however, the events we experience in life allow us to become enlightened about ourselves and other people. The enlightenment we receive helps us evolve in our journey as spiritual beings because we are able to come to an understanding of the human condition and the importance of love, forgiveness, and compassion in triumphing over adversity.

I believe the ultimate enlightenment to be achieved is the knowledge that we are all gods and goddesses, children of the Most High God, and we are responsible for learning how to co-create to bring heaven on earth and to use our God-given power to manifest love, beauty, joy, and wholeness. Thus, our ultimate objective in enlightenment is to know who we are and to remember the power that the Godhead has given us to transform harmful conditions into beneficial ones.

I came by my abilities honestly; both my mother and my father had abilities. My mother was what I like to refer to as a "closet psychic." She revealed her psychic impressions to only a handful of family members. On the other hand, my father was very open about his abilities, especially his visions. I attribute his openness regarding his psychic abilities to being half-Native American. I didn't have his influence growing up because my parents were divorced from the time I was a baby. I never remember them ever being together. I recall my mother receiving most of her messages and impressions through dreams.

There was one time in particular when she received a visit from the spirit of one of her first cousins, Jake, who had just died on impact from a car accident. I recall her saying that she woke up immediately after his visit and looked over at the alarm clock—it was two a.m. At about seven o'clock that morning, she told my grandmother about her dream. One hour later, my grandmother received a phone call from Jake's mother telling her that he had died about two o'clock that morning in an automobile accident. My grandmother replied, "Yes, I know; Phyllis had a visit from him right after he passed. Jake told Phyllis to tell you not to worry; he is in a good place and at peace."

My mother also had a healing gift. Her mother was

frying chicken one afternoon when I heard a scream that made my blood curdle. I ran into the kitchen just in time to witness my mother hovering her hands over my grandmother's chest while silently mouthing some words. I have no idea what she was saying, but I felt it was magical. I watched as the redness from the grease burn dissipated from my grandma's chest. Once the healing session was over, my mother became aware of my presence, which seemed to startle her. I asked her how she healed my grandmother. She replied, "I can't tell you. If I do, I won't be able to do it anymore." She went on to say she would tell me before she died, but she never did. She took the secret with her to the grave.

I often wonder why she couldn't or wouldn't tell me. I concluded that she may have been afraid of being branded a witch or accused of practicing witchcraft. I guess the days of the witch hunt are really not that far away. In the past, women, in particular, were always extremely cautious about sharing their abilities. Three hundred years might seem like a long time ago, but accounts of witch trials still thread through family histories, both in the United States and throughout Europe. Even now, in certain African countries, being accused of witchcraft can result in torture and death, with mothers and grandmothers ripped from their families. Fortunately, these days, not as many people feel the need to remain secretive about having psychic and healing abilities. When I was growing up, we definitely kept our abilities a secret.

According to the Pew Forum on Religious and Public Life's 2008 Religious Landscape, even though the U.S. is still predominantly Christian, many people "blend Christianity with Eastern or New Age beliefs such as reincarnation, astrology, and the presence of spiritual energy in physical objects. Sizable minorities of all major U.S. religious groups say they have experienced supernatural phenomena, such as being in touch with the dead or with ghosts." Although many people are now blending Christian and Eastern spiritual beliefs, some traditional Christian denominations still condemn Eastern spiritual beliefs and the gifts of God, such as healing, psychism, and mediumship.

Jesus Christ had all three of the aforementioned abilities. Everywhere Jesus went, he healed as many people as he could. He counseled people by using his psychic ability, including the woman at the well. He used his mediumship ability to talk with Moses and Elijah on the Mount of Transfiguration, and they had been dead for centuries. Mediumship is nothing more than the gift of discerning spirits. The discerning of spirits is just one of the many gifts given by the Spirit, as noted in the *First Epistle to the Corinthians,* chapter twelve, verses four through ten (KJV):

> *Now there are diversities of gifts, but the same Spirit. And there are differences in administrations, but the same Lord.*
>
> *And there are diversities of operations, but it is the same God who works all in all.*

But the manifestation of the Spirit is given to every man for his own profit.

For to one is given by the Spirit the word of wisdom; to another the word of knowledge by the same Spirit;

To another faith by the same Spirit; to another the gifts of healing by the same Spirit;

To another, the working of miracles

To another prophecy:

To another discerning spirit:

To another, divers kinds of tongues; To another, the interpretation of tongues

Throughout the years, I have had many friends and acquaintances who believed that God no longer demonstrates His power on earth through individuals. In the second book of Timothy, verse 3:5 warns against associating with individuals who have a form of religion or godliness but deny its power. I have listed several different translations below for your consideration:

Having a form of godliness but denying the power thereof, from such turn away. The King James Version

They will act religious, but they will reject the power that

could make them godly. Stay away from people like that! New Living Translation.

They will hold to an outward form of godliness but deny its power. Stay away from such people. International Standard Version

Having a form of piety but denying the power of it; and from these turn away. Darby Bible Translation

What is a form of godliness? It is the practice of abiding by the ordinances of religion as demonstrated by religious activity. The resultant activity is performed within the parameters of human power and does not require any supernatural or spiritual power. The gifts of the Spirit mentioned earlier are not utilized. It is possible to be intensely active in the outside work of the church and yet know nothing of spiritual power. You could be an eloquent preacher or Sunday school teacher and know nothing of the mysterious power of the Spirit.

From what I understand, although my grandmother's parents were Catholic, she was encouraged to attend a local Protestant church because there were no Catholic churches near her rural home. Like her parents, she made sure her children and grandchildren all attended church. Many of my grandmother's friends were very religious. I remember making the mistake of giving my grandma a message from the spirit of one of her older brothers in front of her friend Rose. Rose was super religious and believed that all psychic abilities came from the Devil.

My great-uncle Joe had just visited me in a vision and told me to tell Nora he would be leaving soon and not to worry because he would be able to wear his shoes again. Upon delivering the message, Rose reprimanded me on the spot. Her comments were very hurtful, especially when she said, "You stop that; that comes from the devil, and you are a witch. That's Satanism." My reply to her was, "I am neither a witch nor a Satanist. I love God, and I go to Sunday School every week." I was about twelve years old when that happened, and it had a profound impact on me that stayed with me for a long time. At that moment, I realized I would have to be careful about what I said in front of people outside my own family. I'll talk more about the visitations I received from her siblings later in the book.

Whereas my mother received many of her impressions in dreams, my father received most of his impressions in a fully conscious state. I remember him telling me about some of his visions. One vision in particular bothered me. He described seeing what he called *a little couple* at the foot of his bed the night before. He said that they were there to get his help in delivering a message to their children. However, this *little couple* was dressed in what he described as 17th-century clothing. When I was a young adult, due to my nursing background, I often wondered if he might be schizophrenic because he experienced such lucid visual and auditory impressions. He was, however, always able to distinguish between reality and his impressions, so I concluded that he was just extremely psychic. I remember being filled with trepidation every time I introduced one of my friends to him for fear that he would start talking about his impressions. Looking back, I now realize just how gifted he was.

As I said earlier, I was nine years old when spirits started to come to me to share their messages. At this age, I also experienced my first earthbound spirit. I state that it was *earthbound* because it appeared to me as a full-bodied apparition. It looked so solid, I thought someone had broken into our house. I was on my way upstairs and happened to glance up at the top landing. Standing there in the hallway by the side rail and overlooking the stairwell was a slender, dark-haired man about 5'7". He looked down on me with a menacing grin. I ran down the stairs as quickly as I could without breaking my neck and found my mother in the kitchen, where I promptly reported that an intruder had broken into our house. With urgency in her voice, my mother ordered me to get my brother and go outside. I found my brother in the living room watching television and told him we had to go outside immediately because a stranger had broken into our house.

We were outside for a grand total of five minutes before my somewhat irritated mother appeared. I asked her if she had called the police.

She said, "No, because there is no one in the house. You and your brother need to come in; we're going to be eating soon."

I refused to go in, stating, "I know he's still in there! He's hiding, and you just don't see him! Momma, please don't go back in there. He'll get you."

She allowed me to stay outside while everyone else was

eating dinner. She said, "I'll save your dinner for you, but you'll have to come in before dark."

Later that evening, we visited my Aunt Mertie, who lived a few blocks away. As I watched television in another room, I overheard Momma telling Aunt Mertie about the invisible intruder at home. I recall my Aunt Mertie saying something about the book of Corinthians and the gifts of the spirit.

Much later in my development, I realized that the apparition I saw leaning over the railing was actually an earthbound spirit. Most of the time, earthbound spirits initiate communication with me in a very physical way by making me see them or feel their presence. The most common way they let me know they are present and want to communicate is by making me feel chills or making me go cold on the side of my body where they're standing. For instance, if one is standing on my left side, then the whole left side of my body will grow icy cold to the core from the center of my body to the periphery. Another way earthbound spirits make me aware of their presence is by touch. I might perceive their touch as a spider web-type sensation on my face, arms, or legs. Sometimes they make me feel the pressure of their hand on my head, shoulder, arms, or legs.

Some earthbound spirits don't necessarily want to communicate with me, but I am made aware of their presence. Usually, if an earthbound spirit is present, I can sense it watching me. If one is present but trying to hide from me, my guide, Yeshua, will let me know so I can attempt to cross it over. Although I can perceive and communicate with earthbound spirits, I prefer to receive healing messages from loved ones that have already crossed over and are in the loving light of the Great Spirit.

~ Two ~

SPIRITS INVADE MY DREAMS

> *Trust in dreams, for in them is hidden the gate to eternity.*
> Kahlili Gibran (1883-1931). *On Death.*

Macy's Last Wish

Macy was a tall, slender, mature woman about five feet, seven inches tall, and weighing a hundred and thirty pounds. Her look was distinctive, with green eyes, pale skin, and flaming red hair. Extremely extroverted with a straightforward and sometimes sarcastic personality, she could be laughing and bubbly one minute and cussing you out with her Texan accent the next. She was a prankster and also loved telling jokes. Macy never called me by my name; she had her own name for me, *little girl*. Macy and I worked together as nurses on the same unit occasionally. Ironically, the last time we worked together, Macy made the following comment to me:

If I ever get in the same condition as that woman in room 205, I hope someone will just take a shotgun and shoot me. I have a living will that states that if I have any kind of brain damage that puts me in a coma, it is my wish that all treatment and nourishment be withheld. I refuse to end up a vegetable trapped in a body like that poor woman. Her family should just take her off the vent and let her go.

Macy's comments made me shudder. I quickly rebuked her by saying, "Macy, that's awful; you shouldn't say such things. There is always hope!"

Macy turned to me and said with a serious expression, "I mean it!"

At the time, I didn't realize just how prophetic her statements were until two weeks later when she visited me in a dream. In this dream, I walked into a patient room where Macy was lying in a hospital bed with her eyes closed. I started to give her a tube feeding through a nasogastric tube when she opened her eyes, sat straight up in bed, looked at me, and sternly said, "Little girl, what in the hell do you think you're doing?"

I immediately dropped the tube feeding, turned, and ran out of the room screaming. Jolted awake by my own screaming, I was totally shaken by what I had just dreamed.

Three days after the dream, my nursing manager approached me and said that Macy had been hit by a car while walking to her mailbox and that she was being assigned to me. She went on to say that Macy had spent the last three days in the ICU and was being moved to our med-surg unit for comfort care. She explained that

Macy had a living will, which stated that she wanted to die naturally without heroics or interventions of any kind in the event she succumbed to any illness or injury that put her in a vegetative state. Her living will stipulated that all life-sustaining interventions, including total parenteral nutrition, tube feedings, and intravenous fluids, must be withheld. Macy had been in a coma ever since the accident. She had a severe closed head injury and brain swelling, which resulted in irreversible brain damage. The doctors believed she would remain in a coma indefinitely. Even if she came out of the coma, she would remain in a vegetative state.

The dream visitation I received from Macy's spirit was the confirmation I needed to care for her while she passed naturally with only comfort measures. Without the dream, I would have been uncomfortable allowing Macy to die. Up until that time, I believed it was unethical not to try to save a physical life because there's always hope. I can sense Macy's spirit looking over my shoulder as I write about her. I can hear her saying to me, "Little girl, make sure you get it right!" God bless you, Macy. I know your spirit lives on!

The Desecration

Every year on the Fourth of July, the city of Wilmington launches fireworks from the *Battleship North Carolina*, and spectators line up to sit by the Cape Fear River. It's a very festive event with vendors, music, beer, wine, and party favors appropriate for the Fourth. My husband, Michael, who is now deceased, and I attended the 4th of July event in Wilmington the year before our unplanned tour of the Bellamy Mansion. I fell so much in love with the charm of the riverfront during our first trip to Wilmington that I started entertaining thoughts of buying a house there, becoming a permanent resident, and never leaving. It was during my ghostly tour of the Bellamy Mansion that I discovered I wasn't the only one who wanted to reside in Wilmington and never leave. One year later, my ghostly tour would be validated by an actual, unplanned tour.

On the day of our unplanned tour, I woke up just before dawn and could not fall back to sleep. Back then, I worked every other weekend at the hospital, and it was my scheduled weekend off, so I had planned to sleep late that morning, at least until eight o'clock. However, the weird energy I was perceiving was not going to allow me to sleep. Instead, it was making me feel compelled to go to Wilmington. I felt we should drive down, have lunch on the Cape Fear Riverfront, and then return home. Because I was unable to sleep, I got out of bed and made myself a cup of coffee. When Michael got up a couple of hours later, I told him that I wanted to go to Wilmington and have lunch on the riverfront. It was very unusual for us to take unplanned trips, as we were not spontaneous people by nature. Michael agreed to the trip, and we left within the hour. The drive down was very pleasant, and we arrived in less than two hours.

After a leisurely lunch by the riverside, we started the trip back home. We were only a few blocks from the riverfront when I happened to look up from my book just in time to see the mansion that had been in my dream two weeks earlier. As we drove by, I told my husband that we needed to find a restaurant or convenience store with travel brochures for Wilmington. I told him we had just passed a house on the left-hand side of the road that I had dreamed of, and I wanted to find information about it. We ended up at the local library just a few blocks down the road. As soon as we entered the library, we encountered a rack immediately to our right that was full of brochures. Sure enough, they had a brochure with a picture of the mansion in my dream—the Bellamy Mansion—and they were giving tours that very day. We turned around and drove back to the house. We had about thirty minutes before the next tour, so I thought it would be a good time to share my dream. I told Michael where we would find everything and what I learned about the history of the mansion straight from Eliza, the lady of the house. In order to tell Eliza's story, I have to go back a couple of weeks and explain the visitation I had from her in my dream.

Before having my dream, I had never seen this mansion and had no prior knowledge about it. Even in the dream, I didn't know it was the Bellamy Mansion, nor did I know it was located in Wilmington, North Carolina. Anyway, the dream began with a tour of the carriage house, followed by the slave quarters, grounds, small gardens, and finally the mansion. Although I initially could not see my tour guide, I could feel her powerful presence. I perceived her to be a strong, no-nonsense kind of woman who knew how to get things done. This spirit had not crossed over and was still residing in the house. She gave me my own private tour while explaining pertinent information for each area outside the house as well as every room inside the house.

While on this tour, I received a history lesson I will never forget. After touring the outside areas of the property, I was guided down a sidewalk that led to a flight of stairs and the huge back porch of the house. I looked up and noticed that there were two winding staircases on each end of the porch. My invisible guide told me these were the servant stairs and that servants were not allowed to use the main staircase within the house.

Upon entering the backdoor, I noticed a long, wide hallway with a grand staircase to my right. There were four large rooms on this level, with two situated on each side of the hallway. The front door was located directly across from me on the other side of the house. My invisible guide led me into the large room immediately to my right, which was located in the back of the house. She told me that this was the room where they took care of business. This room had wallpaper with a large floral print on what seemed to be a burgundy background. As I looked around the room, I noticed that the wallpaper started to burn and peel away from the wall. After witnessing the fire, I was shown the room again, and it was completely restored with similar wallpaper but a different floral print. A female voice boomed throughout the room and exclaimed, "I made sure this room did not burn, and I also saw to it that it was completely restored!"

I was then guided into the adjoining room located in the front of the house and told this was the sitting room for the women to congregate, talk, and work on their stitchery. I was made aware of the long windows that extended from ceiling to floor on the front and sides of the house. The sun streamed brightly through each window, filling the room with iridescent light. The luminous room gave me a warm and happy feeling. My attention was drawn to one of the windows on the side of the house. I walked over to the window and looked out. In the middle of the road was a beautiful, ornate water fountain. It seems as if I stood there for hours just watching as the water splashed into the large basin below. The sound of the running water mesmerized me. I could also smell river water as it wafted through the open window on a warm, gentle breeze. I detected the scent of roses and noticed there were several red rose vines scattered about the side yard. When I turned away from the window, I saw two women sitting on an elegant sofa and another one sitting in an armchair next to the sofa. The mood seemed to be light and happy. They laughed and talked amongst themselves as they worked on their embroidery and cross-stitch projects. I knew I was an observer, and they could not see me. I found myself wishing I could have been sitting alongside them, joining in the conversation, and working on my own stitchery.

I was then led back into the hallway and up the stairs to the second floor, where I was shown all of the bedrooms on both sides of the house. My guide made sure I saw the huge bathroom that showcased a large bathtub and chamber pots encased in a wooden cabinet. As I inspected the bathroom, I was told that everyone received a tub bath at least once a week because cleanliness is next to godliness. After touring the second floor, we climbed the stairs to the third floor. Upon reaching the top landing, I heard the laughter and giggles of young children. My eyes were drawn to a stage at the far end of the room, where several of the older children were putting on a show for the younger children. I was informed that this was where the children stayed and played because children should be seen and not heard.

Next on the tour were the dining room and kitchen, located in the basement. After descending several flights of stairs, I entered the dining room first. In the center of this room stood a long oak table. The ornate chairs accompanying this table appeared to be made of the same kind of wood. Velvet material covered the back and seats of these chairs, but I can't recall the color. I passed through the door on the other side of the dining room to enter the spacious kitchen area. On the far side of the wall across from the entrance leading into the kitchen from the dining room stood a big cast iron wood stove. In the center of the kitchen was a large food preparation table with several bowls of fruit and vegetables on it.

Once the tour of the kitchen was over, I found myself on the first floor again. I was standing in the hallway at the entrance to the second parlor room, located across from the first parlor room, where I saw the ladies sitting and working on their stitchery. I had not been in this room before. Standing with her back towards me, I saw a lady with dark hair pulled up into a large bun. She was wearing a beautiful, bell-shaped navy blue velvet dress that fit snugly around her waist. She appeared to be chastising a group of soldiers who were standing by a grand, white marble fireplace. Several of these men had their elbows resting on the mantlepiece. They were apparently enjoying the warmth produced by the intense, blazing fire. Several more men were hanging out in a smaller room at the rear of the big parlor room, which was separated by a partition with a wide entryway. Some of them were gathered around what looked like a piano but sounded like a harpsichord. A man with red hair was playing this instrument while the other men formed a semicircle around him, drinking, singing, and laughing.

The most significant man in my dream was the officer standing at the far left end of the fireplace. He had shoulder-length, strawberry blonde hair with a matching beard. I remember thinking he was short for a man, and he was also very thin. I knew immediately, however, that he was a very important officer and in charge of all the other men. He was chewing tobacco, which he frequently spat out onto the beautiful white marble hearth. Eliza politely asked this officer to stop spitting on the hearth. Revealing his brown, tobacco-stained teeth, he grinned and told her to shut her mouth or she would be arrested. With a sarcastic but calm tone of voice, Eliza told the officer that he didn't have any manners and that he must have been raised in a barn. The men standing around the fireplace laughed in response to her comment and then intentionally took turns spitting their wads of tobacco onto the hearth. After witnessing the behavior of these soldiers, Eliza responded by stating in a calm but matter-of-fact voice, "Ya'll are nothing but a bunch of barbarians!"

I noticed that the door to the front entrance, which was situated to my right, was open, and there was a man in a carriage who was waiting for Eliza. Then it occurred to me that these men had taken possession of the house, and the owners had to stay away for their own safety. I heard the man who was waiting in the carriage with the reins in his hands yell out, "Eliza, come on! We've got to go!"

She replied, "Okay, I'll be there in a few minutes." On her way towards the front door, she paused to acknowledge me and said, "Hello, my name is Eliza. Welcome to my home."

I remember asking her, "Who are these men?"

She replied, "These men are the damn Yankees who have confiscated my home. They have no right to be here, and now I have to leave because they won't give my home back. I shouldn't have to lose my home. This war is not my fault. It's the men's fault. I'm glad the slaves are free, but these damn Yankees have no right to kick me out of my own home!"

She rushed through the door and boarded the carriage. I watched as the carriage quickly disappeared out of my sight into the silent darkness of the night.

After experiencing some type of time-lapse, I found myself back in the parlor room that had been occupied by the Yankee soldiers. The once beautiful and pristine-looking fireplace and hearth were now covered in varying shades of brown stains, no doubt a result of the copious amounts of spittle it received from the *barbarians.* Eliza, the woman I had seen earlier in the beautiful blue velvet dress, was now wearing a cotton dress with a pinafore-type apron. She was on her hands and knees with a bucket of soapy water at her side. She seemed to be swearing at her long-gone offenders as she scrubbed back and forth with a large, wooden, stiff-bristled brush. Obviously, she was upset about the squalid condition of her home. As she tried to hold back the tears, she said to me, "John was able to get our home back, but look at it; those barbarians have just about destroyed it. The floors and walls are filthy, and the beautiful fireplaces are ruined. Those damn Yankees have desecrated my home! I lost my home once, and I will never lose it again. I will restore it, and I will never be made to leave again, not ever!" She went on to say:

> *Please let everybody know that I never wished harm to anyone. I was happy when the slaves were emancipated. I don't believe anyone should be a slave, not black or white. It was the men's fault. I was just as much a slave as anyone else. I was a woman, which placed me in the same category as chattel. I was subservient to all the men, including my sweet, loving husband. I had no vote, choice, or voice in the world. I want to set the record straight: although I benefited from slavery, I had no power as a woman in the South to openly defy it without enduring serious consequences. I know there were more important issues at stake during the war than losing my home. If loving my home is a sin, then I am guilty as charged. The love that I have for my home has nothing to do with*

> *war or slavery. My home in Wilmington was a sanctuary for me when I was alive. Now, it's a sanctuary for my soul.*

I could feel the sadness and sense of helplessness Eliza felt concerning her inability to do anything about slavery in her time. Her words: "It's the men's fault. I'm glad the slaves are free" played over and over again in my mind.

When I finished telling Michael about my dream, I glanced into the rearview mirror and noticed several cars had pulled in behind us. The guide had also arrived and was waiting on the steps of the back porch for us to begin the tour. This time it would be given by a physical person that I could see and hear with my physical eyes and ears. The tour eerily started in the same manner as my dream tour with the spirit of Eliza. We toured the left side (if you're facing the house) of the first level, starting with the wallpapered room that caught fire in the early 1970s. Our tour guide, Sally, told us that this room had been used as a study. I remembered what Eliza had said about this room being used to conduct business. Our tour guide explained that it was a miracle that somehow the fire department was alerted just in time to contain the fire and keep it from spreading to the rest of the house. She said, fortunately, the fire caused mostly smoke damage and not much physical damage. From the back room, we entered the parlor room, where I had watched as the ladies of the house worked on their stitchery. We left the parlor room and ascended the stairs immediately to our left. We toured the second floor, where the bathroom and bedrooms were located. I didn't get a lecture on this tour about cleanliness being next to godliness, as I did on Mrs. Bellamy's tour. What I did learn is that the family did not spend a lot of time on this floor. From the second floor, we ascended the steps to the third floor. This floor contained a stage and other play areas where the children entertained each other. Eliza told me on her tour that the children played on this floor because children should be seen and not heard. We also didn't get that information on this tour.

From the top floor, we descended the steps until we came to the dining room and kitchen areas in the basement. The actual dining room seemed smaller than the one I saw in my dream. The kitchen was exactly as I remembered it. From the kitchen, we ascended the steps to the first floor, touring the remaining rooms on the right-hand side of the house. We viewed the front parlor room, where I had witnessed Eliza's encounter with the Yankee soldiers as they defiled her beautiful marble hearth. From the front parlor room, we entered the adjoining room, where I had seen the Yankee soldiers gathered around the harpsichord, singing and drinking. Sally said the Yankee officers spent most of their time during the occupation in these two parlor rooms. She said that they preferred this room over the other parlor room because of the adjoining music room. Our tour with Sally came to an end. Although I felt that the actual tour was less informative than the one Eliza gave me, it did validate much of what Eliza had said on her tour. Ironically, the physical tour with Sally took the same route as the ghost tour with Mrs. Bellamy. Wow! That's spooky.

It's my opinion that Eliza came to me in a dream because of her need to let people know how she really felt in her heart about slavery, which—because of societal expectations—may not have been what she projected while she was alive. I think she felt she had to go along with what was expected of her because she was a woman and had no vote, choice, or voice in the world, and although she was happy for the slaves when they were emancipated, it may have been unacceptable for her to say so at the time. She also made it perfectly clear to me that she has been protecting her home ever since she returned to it after the War Between the States. Because of her intervening influence, the mansion has been restored and will remain a landmark for centuries to come. She also made it very clear to me that she would never leave her home again. Not even to cross over. The spirit of Mrs. Bellamy is still at home in her mansion.

Casper, The Voyeuristic Host

At the last minute, my husband, Michael, and I were invited to accompany his brother and sister-in-law to the home of a friend of theirs for the weekend. Neither my husband nor I knew the Worths, but we were happy to get away to the coast for a couple of days. As we were pulling into the driveway after a nearly three-hour drive, I began to feel an overwhelming presence emanating from the house. It felt somewhat familiar as if I had somehow encountered it before. We walked up the sidewalk and ascended the short set of steps to the porch. We tapped the ornate door knocker, and as soon as Mrs. Worth opened the front door, I got a glimpse of the staircase leading upstairs to the second floor. I immediately recognized exactly where I was. I remembered the dream that I had about a week earlier. I whispered to my husband, who was standing on my left side, This is the home of Casper, the friendly host. That's right, I said host, not ghost. However, this notion would turn out to be incorrect. To tell you this story, I have to describe the dream.

My dream began with me ascending the stairs and, at the top, being greeted by a spirit that quickly appeared to me out of nowhere. He looked like a solid white cloud with a big head, a round body, and no legs. He reminded me of the cartoon character Casper. He didn't tell me his name, but with excitement in his voice, he said, "Welcome to my home!"

He quickly wisped around me like a foggy mist, leading me from room to room while explaining the function of each room before we saw it. A whole apartment existed on the upstairs level with three bedrooms, two bathrooms, a kitchen, and a laundry room.

Casper stated in a bragging tone of voice, "We had the whole upstairs transformed into an apartment. It's nice, isn't it?"

I turned around to reply, but he was no longer there. He had vanished as quickly as he had appeared. The dream was over.

As soon as my husband and I reached the landing on the second floor, I said to him, "Come on, I'll give you the tour." I gave my tour by describing each room before entering it, in the same fashion that Casper had given me his tour. At the conclusion of my little tour, my husband was dumbfounded, while I felt a sense of pride, probably much like my original tour guide.

Michael asked me, "Have you been here before?"

I replied, "No, only in my dream."

He shook his head and stated, "You definitely have a gift!"

We put our luggage in our assigned room and went downstairs to join our living host, Mrs. Worth, who was sitting in the parlor room with Michael's brother and sister-in-law. Because it was still early afternoon and a beautiful spring day, we all agreed to take a nature walk on the boardwalk of the sweetwater swamp that was a block away. The sun was shining brightly. The fragrance of magnolias, dogwoods, azaleas, wisteria, and gardenias permeated the air with their sweetness. The mood of our group was lighthearted and fun. As we toured the swamp from the boardwalk, we all laughed heartily while sharing stories and exchanging jokes. We walked for several hours and finally made it back to Casper's house just before dark. That night, we barbecued steaks and chicken in the backyard while we sat around a large stone fire pit, drinking beer and telling more jokes. It had been a wonderful evening full of laughter.

Around 11 p.m., the fun came to an end, and everyone decided to retire for the evening. As soon as my husband and I entered our bedroom, I once again became aware of a familiar presence. Casper, our invisible host, was there. I asked him to leave and explained to him that we were going to bed. Casper did not honor my request and made it clear to me that he was not going to leave. I could feel him a few inches from my face, staring me down. I perceived that he was excited at the prospect of seeing me undress and shower. My original plan was to take a shower and crawl into bed next to my husband; however, Casper altered that plan with his incessant voyeurism and refusal to leave the room. I tried my best to put my gown on without exposing myself. That was a first for me. I accomplished this feat by putting my gown on over my t-shirt and taking my shirt, bra, and jeans off under my gown. I immediately jumped into bed and pulled the covers up under my chin. I got as close to my husband as I could, and I maintained physical contact with him all night long. I stayed awake the whole night, praying for God to make Casper go away.

I was so relieved when the sun finally streamed through the window-laden room. I could feel the atmosphere of the room change with the dawning of the new day. The room took on a wholesome and inviting feeling, as if to say, *Stay; this is a nice place to be.* I was determined that I would not stay in that house fifteen minutes longer, much less another day. Even with the inviting smells of coffee and bacon coming from the downstairs kitchen, I was determined to leave as soon as possible. As soon as my husband stirred from his sleep, I adamantly announced to him that we had to leave immediately. I didn't worry about my makeup that morning. I just wanted to get out of there. Once dressed, we grabbed our luggage and headed down. We found Mrs. Worth in the kitchen, where she was joyfully making breakfast for everyone. I told her that we had to go. She asked why we had to leave so soon and if we could at least stay for breakfast.

Without thinking, I abruptly blurted out, "We have to leave because your house is haunted! But there is something that I don't understand. Why is it that your husband seems to be haunting the upstairs and not the downstairs?"

She looked at me in amazement and said, "I always thought he was still here. When he was alive, we lived in the upstairs apartment and rented out the downstairs. After he died, I started living downstairs and closed off the upstairs because of the things that were happening up there."

I asked her, "What kind of things?"

She replied, "Well, things would go missing or get moved around. There was also a lot of banging and noises up there, so I moved downstairs, where it seems to be a lot quieter."

I told her that I could understand why she would want to move downstairs and that I certainly would not stay upstairs any longer than I had to. We thanked Mrs. Worth for her hospitality and told her that except for Mr. Worth's behavior, we enjoyed our visit with her. I never recalled being as happy to leave a place as I was to leave that house. At the time, I was not an expert at dealing with obnoxious entities. That wouldn't happen until later in my development when I took my gift more seriously and learned how to properly use it. I also learned that you can't judge a ghost by its appearance. What I thought was Casper the friendly host turned out to be Casper the scary ghost.

The Warning

On a cold and clear winter's night, while deep in sleep, I had a dream that would prove to be a harbinger of things to come within just a few short days. In the dream, I was driving my little red Nissan on an old highway during a snowstorm. I was downshifting when, all of a sudden, my car began to roll and eventually landed upright. As I was struggling to get out of the car, a deep, booming voice, which seemed to come from everywhere, made the statement, "Be still and know that I am God." Then I saw a big hand come through the sunroof, which lifted me up and out of the car.

A few days later, my husband, Michael, called me from work and asked me if I wanted to meet him at a local restaurant for lunch. I was off duty at the hospital that day and free to join him. As I spoke with him, I remembered the dream I had just a few days earlier. While I had Michael on the phone, I told him about the dream. He reassured me that nothing would happen to me because the latest weather report called for six to eight inches of snow, which wouldn't start until later that evening. At that time, there was no snow on the ground, so I agreed to go ahead and meet him for lunch; however, I still had an intense feeling of foreboding and dread. I was to meet Michael at about 12:30 p.m., so I left the house at noon. At approximately 12:05 p.m., it started to snow. Ten minutes later, the road was completely covered. Underneath the snow was a patchy layer of black ice, which had accumulated from the sleet and freezing rain that had fallen the night before. I started to panic on the inside, even though I was determined to remain calm. I told myself that even if I did have an accident in the snow that day, my dream indicated that I would be rescued by divine intervention and that I would be okay.

Sure enough, within a few minutes, two cars in front of me hit a patch of black ice and ended up in the ditch on the right-hand side of the road. Before I had time to react, I also hit the same patch of ice. In an attempt to avoid hitting the cars in the ditch, I tried to correct my skid but ended up in the left lane with my front end facing the median and the rear end in the right lane. As I looked up, I saw a huge GMC truck sliding uncontrollably toward me. I knew he was trying to stop but was unable to do so. A small voice in my head said, "Lay down across the console. It will be alright." I did as the voice instructed me to do. As soon as I lay across the console, I felt the impact of the GMC truck as it t-boned me on the driver's side. I heard metal crunching, but I was untouched. Because I had moved away from the door by lying across the console, I was able to avoid the door crushing me. As soon as everything came to a standstill, I crawled over to the passenger seat and let myself out of the door on that side. Once outside, I met with the driver of the GMC truck, who happened to be an off-duty police officer. He didn't sustain any injuries either, not even a scratch. We were both okay, but shaken. I truly felt that the dream I had several nights earlier gave me the faith to know that everything would work out okay. My car was totaled, but I didn't have a scratch on me, nor did I have any aches or pains that day or afterward. I am thankful for the divine guidance and protection given to me that day.

~ Three ~

SPIRITS IN THE ASTRAL

*I've been walking through the middle of nowhere,
Trying to get to heaven before they close the door.*
—Bob Dylan. *Trying to Get to Heaven* (song),
1997.

The Fire Starter

For several days, I had been feeling worried about the little elderly lady who lived next door to me. Although I did not know her personally, I felt an intense burden for her. I watched through the sliding glass door of my living room as she walked to her mailbox each day. There was absolutely no obvious reason why I should feel worried about this lady. There were no outward signs of distress. Her gait was strong and steady. She seemed to be behaving appropriately. Nevertheless, after about a week of constant worry, what I was feeling morphed into a sense of profound foreboding. I knew something bad was going to happen to this lady. I just didn't know what. Upon retiring to bed on the night of the incident, in my prayers, I asked Spirit to either show me what this feeling was about or lift it off me. I just couldn't take it any longer. I needed to get on with my own life and concerns. Immediately after I stated my petition in prayer, I had a vision of an amorphous white cloud that appeared out of nowhere and moved slowly toward me. As it approached, I watched my spirit hop onto this cloud and sail mid-air through the wall of my bedroom into my daughter's bedroom, and then out of her bedroom through the party wall into the apartment next door.

I found myself standing in the bathroom of the elderly woman's apartment. When I looked down at my arms and legs, I noticed that they appeared translucent, but I felt solid. I also noticed that I could see through the walls of the bathroom out into the apartment. As I gazed out of her bathroom through the open door, I saw her bedroom (she had a one-bedroom, one-bathroom, garden-style apartment). My attention was then drawn to my right, where I could see my elderly neighbor through the walls. I watched as she walked from the living room down the narrow hallway, past the kitchen on her right, and then into her bedroom. She meandered over to the nightstand, picked up a pack of cigarettes, lit one, took a puff, crawled into bed, and put the cigarette in a round metal ashtray that she had previously placed in the middle of the bed. She rose up to get out of bed, and when she did, the cigarette popped out of the ashtray and landed on top of the bed covers. Then, she walked back down the hallway into her living room and sat in a recliner situated by the sliding glass door. My attention was once again drawn to the bedroom. I watched as the smoldering mattress erupted in flames, burning from the middle of the bed and spreading outward. As I watched, the flames danced higher and higher, eventually licking the ceiling.

After witnessing the mattress catch fire, I immediately snapped back into my physical body, and my eyes popped open. I was horrified by what I had just witnessed. I was scheduled to take a real estate brokerage exam that morning, so I went ahead and got up earlier than usual. More importantly, I wanted to check and see if there was any merit to my vision. I got out of bed and went into my daughter's room, where I touched the party wall with both hands. I was trying to discern heat, which would verify the validity of my out-of-body experience. I didn't feel any heat. In fact, the wall felt cool. I began to wonder if I might have been dreaming. I thought to myself, *There was no way it was a dream.* It was all so real. I went into the dining room and walked over to the party wall on the far side of the room. This party wall separated my dining room from my neighbor's living room. I ran the palm of my right hand along the wall with a long, sweeping motion from one end to the other. It was cool, just like my daughter's bedroom wall. As I was checking the wall for heat, my husband walked in and asked me what I was doing. I briefly described my out-of-body experience and asked him to go next door to see if the apartment was on fire.

He came back a few minutes later and said, "It's dark in there. I can't see anything."

I sighed with relief and said, "Good, I'm glad there's no fire."

He said, No, Shirley, it's dark in there because of the smoke. Call the fire department."

Filled with trepidation, I was wondering how I was going to explain my knowledge of the fire next door without appearing to be an arsonist. I made the comment to my husband that I hoped the elderly lady was okay. He told me she was not home because her son told him the day before that he was going to take her out to dinner and then back to his house to spend the night. I told my husband I believed she was in the recliner beside the sliding glass door because that was where I had last seen her in my vision. I asked him to please tell the firemen that our neighbor loved to sit in her recliner by the sliding glass door. As soon as the fire trucks arrived, he went out to greet the firemen and let them know that an elderly lady lived in the apartment and that she liked to sit in her chair beside the glass door. As soon as the firefighters slid open the glass door, they found her sitting in her recliner. She was still alive but had severe smoke inhalation.

The firemen quickly extinguished the fire. The Captain said that the fire started because the mattress was ignited by a cigarette. The fire consumed the bedroom and kitchen before it was contained. The master bathroom, where I stood in my spirit body, was spared from the flames but suffered heavy smoke damage. We were fortunate that the fire did not come through the party wall to our apartment; however, the neighbors who lived above our next-door neighbor suffered damage to their dining room and kitchen. Fortunately, they all got out safely. I never saw or heard from my elderly neighbor again. I think her son may have placed her in a nursing facility when she was discharged from the hospital.

My Spirit Needed A Time Out!

On this beautiful spring day, I was off duty from the hospital and bored with nothing special to do, so I decided to watch an LMN movie. I made some popcorn, sat down on the sofa, and turned on the television. I relaxed and curled up into a comfy position. Suddenly, I found myself standing in the middle of the room. It took me a moment to realize that my physical body was still on the couch, while my spirit body was definitely in the middle of the room. Once again, I was having an out-of-body experience. However, this experience was somewhat different from the fire-starter incident ten years earlier.

The sunshine coming through the window panes and glass doors seemed to illuminate every object and piece of furniture in the room. I felt as if I had some kind of superpower vision. My visual acuity was extremely sharp. Colors seemed to pop and vibrate, and I could see for miles and miles without losing focus. I was even able to see through the walls of my house if I wanted to. I also had panoramic vision. I could see 360 Degrees around me without having to turn my body. I could get a microscopic view of anything I wanted to look at just by having the thought that I wanted to see it closely. All I had to do was think about where I wanted to be, and I would be there. For example, my attention was drawn outside to the backyard, and I wanted to go, so I immediately found myself there upon the thought. The sound of the birds chirping came through crystal clear, like a beautiful melody playing in my ears. I was intensely happy and at peace. Everything seemed to be right until my left-sided, analytical brain kicked in and screamed, *Oh no, this is all wrong! This isn't right! Shirley, come back! Shirley, come back! Shirley, come back now!* On that last command from my brain to my spirit, my eyes popped open, and I sprung up off the couch, trying to figure out what had just happened to me. I wondered if I had actually died. I even checked my pulse for a full minute to see if I had any arrhythmias. What could have caused my spirit to wander outside my body? To this day, I still don't have the answer to why I had this experience. I guess my spirit just needed a time-out!

The Shadow Man In My House

I have seen shadow people before, especially in the ICU, where I worked as a critical care nurse. This particular shadow man, however, seemed far more menacing, in part because it was in my house. On a sunny, warm day in August, I had just folded a load of laundry and started upstairs to put it away. About halfway up the stairs, I glanced up and saw the profile of a solid black entity in the form of a man. He was wearing a wide-brimmed hat similar to the one worn by the man on the Quaker Oats cereal box. This entity seemed to be moving slower than the other shadow people that I had seen. I watched as he slowly walked across the landing at the top of the stairs. He moved from right to left and entered my bedroom. This shadow figure had a profile like a man but no detailed facial features. He had legs with no feet and moved as if he were walking with a normal gait. I couldn't seem to wrap my head around the fact that I was actually seeing a shadow man in my house. I called out to it, thinking that maybe it was my brother, Ralph, who I was seeing. I asked him, "Why are you going into my bedroom?"

Of course, I didn't get a reply. I ran into my bedroom, then into my bathroom, followed by my closet. No one was there! I crept across the hallway and lightly knocked on the door to Ralph's bedroom. He didn't answer, so I cracked the door open and looked in. He was stretched across the bed, sound asleep, and snoring loudly. I called out to my husband for help. I ran down the stairs and grabbed the sage and lighter out of the china cabinet. As soon as the sage was lit and burning, I started filling every nook and cranny of every room downstairs, beginning in the kitchen, proceeding to the laundry room, the bathroom, then the dining room, and lastly, the living room. As I walked around each room, I commanded all negative entities to leave and for love and light to fill each room. After the downstairs was completely saged, I climbed the stairs with my husband closely behind me and continued saging while stating my commands.

I proceeded to the upstairs hall bathroom and then to the office. I cleaned all three bedrooms, saving the one that Ralph was using for last. I flung the door open and found him still lying across the bed, passed out. Apparently, he had been drinking again to excess. As I fanned the smoking sage and recited my prayers, Ralph began to stir from his alcohol-induced coma. He started to giggle and mock me by saying, "Love and light, ha ha ha; love and light, ha, ha, ha; love and light; ha, ha, ha." I immediately told him to shut up, but he continued with his stuporous mockery. Soon afterward, Ralph sat up in bed and asked me what was going on. I explained to him that I had just seen a shadow man, but he was gone now. I have often wondered if what I saw was an entity that had attached itself to my brother and was just roaming the house while Ralph slept off his alcohol.

The Ghoul

Just because I'm a medium doesn't mean that I am immune to feeling scared. Dealing with the dead in the astral realm can be downright scary. Although I have never backed down from a spirit, I have had my share of frightening experiences because of them. One of the most frightening experiences was a visitation from a ghost who had not crossed over. This was the ghost of a patient I had been assigned to care for on the telemetry unit for the past two days. I had just crawled into bed, turned out the light, and pulled the bed covers up around my neck when this ghoulish-looking head without a body floated in mid-air about three feet in front of me. I recognized the face as belonging to a patient I had taken care of the day before;

however, her appearance had changed dramatically from the last time I saw her. She had long, brittle gray hair and gaping holes where her eyes and mouth should have been.

I immediately closed my eyes and started to pray when it occurred to me that I had nothing to be afraid of. This was my patient's way of letting me know that she had passed away and was now a ghost. She didn't say anything to me. She just floated in mid-air for what seemed to be several minutes. I felt this patient was somewhat confused in her death state because she was confused while she was alive. I know I gave her the best care possible. I don't think any other nurse could have done better. I asked the spirit if she saw a light. She turned her head as if she were looking around the room. I told her that her loved ones were waiting for her in the light, and she could be with them if she went into it. As soon as I told her she could be with her loved ones, she disappeared from my sight as quickly as she appeared. I called the hospital the next day and asked if this particular patient had died. I was told that she had died the night before, around 9 p.m. My visitation occurred around 10 p.m.

~ Four ~

SPIRITS ON THE JOB

> *Are not all angels ministering spirits sent to serve those who will inherit salvation?*
> —Hebrews 1:14

Murder At The Office

In the days before returning to nursing school to finish my degree, I worked as a property manager with a large commercial and residential real estate firm. Unlike most of their managers, I had my real estate broker's license and believed I could achieve great success with this company. One of my responsibilities as the property manager of several large apartment communities was to review and close the books at the end of each month. While I was closing the books at one of my largest communities, I experienced the most frightening day of my life. The following is an account of what happened:

This day began much the same as any other. I had my usual cup of coffee and sent my daughter off to school. At the office, I greeted the leasing agent, the maintenance supervisor and his crew, the maid, and the painter as they all filed in to get a cup of coffee and attend the morning meeting. Morning meetings were informal but very effective. We worked together to plan daily activities and offer suggestions for any issues that needed to be resolved. I started working on closing the books immediately after the meeting because they had to be submitted by midnight that day. Since I was making significant progress, I decided to go home and take my lunch break. I had been back to work for about an hour when I heard a male voice in my head say loud and clear, "Call 911!" I stopped, picked up the phone on my desk, and said to myself out loud, "What?" I heard the male voice in my head say once again, "Call 911!" Because this command was a little more insistent than the first one, I was strongly compelled by Spirit to make the call. I reached over, punched in the numbers, and waited for the emergency operator; however, when she finally answered and said, "What is the nature of your emergency?" I froze and hung up because I didn't know what to say. I didn't have a clue why I was calling. As soon as I put the phone down, the male voice came through again and said, "Never mind about the call; get under the desk and pull the chair in behind you!" I replied, "Why should I get under the desk?" The male voice commanded, "Just do it now!" I said, "Okay." I crawled under the desk and pulled the chair in behind me as I was instructed.

After a few minutes of being under the desk, I thought to myself, If someone comes in and sees me squatting under this desk, they are going to think I have lost my mind. As soon as this thought passed, I reached up to push the chair away so I could get out. Fortunately for me, before I could move the chair back, I heard a huge crashing sound followed by a deep, sinister male voice audibly saying, "Get down on the floor and stay there! I'll kill you if you move!"

At that moment, I realized we were being robbed. Although I was horrified at what was happening, I was feeling very grateful for the divine intervention I seemed to be experiencing. Nevertheless, I also felt that if this robber discovered me squatting under the desk, he would kill me. I quietly remained under my desk while a parade of employees filed into the office, one at a time. I listened while each employee was brutally commanded to give up their money and jewelry and to lay face down on the floor. They were told not to move, or they would be killed. After this man robbed my employees, he demanded to know where we kept the rent money. I heard the leasing agent reply:

"We don't accept cash for the rent. Look at the

sign on the front door that says we don't accept cash."

The robber said, "Shut up, you bitch! You're lying!"

The maintenance supervisor chimed in and said, "She's telling the truth. All we have are checks. We don't have any cash."

The robber yelled, "Where're the checks?"

The leasing agent said, "They're in the box on top of the short file cabinet."

The robber walked over to the file cabinet and exclaimed, "There ain't nothing in there! If you don't tell me where the money is, I'm going to kill all of you!"

I could see the feet of the robber as he walked behind my desk, shuffling papers around on top of it. I believe the maintenance supervisor could see my feet under the desk from where he lay because he told the robber that there was nothing on the desk and if there were any checks or money, they would be on the desk in the front office.

I watched as the robber's feet walked away from the desk. He apparently decided to check out the desk in the front office because I heard him say, "Everybody, stay down on the floor or I'll come back in here and kill all of you!"

A few moments after his declaration, I heard a gunshot. I thought that maybe it was a warning shot. I had no idea one of our maintenance men had just been shot and was lying in the hallway with a huge hole in his chest. The evil lowlife who had just robbed the office was now a killer!

The leasing agent had apparently also seen my feet while she was lying on the floor and came around behind the desk to let me know that it was okay to come out and that the robber was long gone. She told me not to enter the hallway because Terry had been shot. I told her I was the manager and it was my responsibility to know what was going on with the employees, and I had CPR certification as well as almost two years of nursing school. If anyone needed to be at Terry's side, I was until the EMS could get there. After assessing Terry's condition, however, I knew he wouldn't make it. He had profuse bleeding from his mouth and nose, as well as a big gaping hole, which was located about four inches left of his sternum, between the third and fourth intercostal spaces. There was no doubt he had a mortal gunshot wound that would lead to a quick death. I stayed by his side, trying to comfort and reassure him as he gurgled on his blood and gasped for breath.

It seemed like an eternity before EMS pulled up to the office. They started to work on Terry as soon as they entered the hallway; however, their attempts to save him were futile. He died in the hallway shortly after EMS arrived, never making it to the hospital.

Terry left behind a loving wife and a seven-year-old

daughter who adored him. I remember Terry coming into the office every afternoon so he could call his daughter once she got home from school. He would always tell her he loved her and would be home soon to help her with her homework. I'm sure that as Terry entered the office that afternoon, the only thing on his mind was making his daily phone call to his daughter. He probably never imagined that some monster would be robbing him of his life as he entered the hallway. Terry is with me as I write this story. He would like to make that phone call to his daughter, but since he can't, he has asked me to give a message to her, hoping that she may read it in this book. The message is as follows:

> *My dearest Marie, I have never left your side. I have always watched over you to guide and protect you. I am sorry I could not be with you as your daddy in a physical body, but I was there all the same. I love you and your children. I am proud of you and the strong woman you have become. I am with your mother now, and we are very happy. I'm sorry for the difficult times you have endured, but I have been there to help you every step of the way. I've witnessed your successes and failures and have watched as you have made your way in life. I love you, my beautiful daughter.*

Tears are streaming down my face as I write these words. Although the names are different, I hope one day Marie will read and personally identify with this message from her father.

The man who robbed us and killed Terry was captured and arrested later that day. We all sighed a breath of relief when the police captured this evil man. I think we were afraid he might come back and kill the rest of us, as he had threatened to do in the office. To the best of my knowledge, the man who robbed Terry of his life is still alive and serving a life sentence in prison. I am hoping he will never be eligible for parole.

A very interesting aspect of this story is the fact that for two weeks before the incident occurred, I was compelled to meditate on and pray Psalm 71 every night before retiring to bed. I believe the following four verses of Psalm 71 (NIV) contain the core message of my meditative prayer:

> *In you, Lord, I have taken refuge; let me never be put to shame.*
>
> *In your righteousness, rescue me and deliver me; turn your ear to me and save me.*
>
> *Be my rock of refuge, to which I can always go; give the command to save me, for you are my rock and my fortress.*
>
> *Deliver me, my God, from the hand of the wicked, from the grasp of those who are evil and cruel.*

Please keep in mind that although I did read the Bible from time to time, I was not in the habit of reading it every night. The fact that I was compelled to pray Psalm 71 for two weeks before the robbery leads me to believe that divine intervention was operating in my life long before the incident occurred. I feel that an unseen force was working on my behalf to protect me by working through me to manifest my protection long before I knew what was to come. Many people call this unseen force God. After this horrific incident, I gave up real estate, returned to nursing school, and completed my BSN. I wasn't able to help save Terry's life that day; however, because I was spared the same fate as Terry, I was able to become a Registered Nurse, which allowed me to help save the lives of others.

The Crash Cart Dilemma

I was working on the med-surg unit of a small county hospital when the crash cart incident occurred. My assignment on this particular day included a day surgery patient who had a Lap Chole (surgery to remove her gallbladder) the day before and had been admitted to 24-hour observation because of intractable nausea, vomiting, and elevated blood pressure. She had a history of high blood pressure, for which she took antihypertensives. On the morning I had her as a patient, her blood pressure returned to baseline and was stabilized. She was, however, unable to tolerate any of her breakfast and required a dose of intravenous Phenergan for nausea. Except for nausea, her a.m. assessment was unremarkable. The small dressings at all five of her abdominal wound sites were dry and intact. There was no abdominal redness, rigidity, heat, or abnormal swelling noted. Her vital signs were within normal limits. Her respirations were even and unlabored. On a scale of one to ten, her abdominal pain level was a three. She denied the presence of pain elsewhere, including in her chest.

In spite of her somewhat normal assessment, I couldn't help but feel something was going to go terribly wrong. She asked about her discharge time, and I told her the doctor would be in later that morning to assess her and write her discharge orders. My assessment of her occurred at about 7:30 that morning. Around 9:30 a.m., she had a room full of visitors and was sitting up in bed, talking, and doing well. Her respirations were even and unlabored. She denied nausea and vomiting and offered no complaints. I walked out of the room feeling as if something still wasn't right. At 10:30 a.m., the doctor called the floor to say he had emergency surgery and would be up there later that afternoon. I wanted to tell him to come to see my patient right away, but there was no evidence I could offer to prove that an urgent visit was indicated. My inner voice screamed out in frustration. What could I do?

I was compelled to put the crash cart by the door outside her room but resisted the temptation because, unless there was an actual code blue in progress, the crash cart was kept in the same place so that we would know where to find it. I just couldn't shake the ominous feeling I was having about this observation patient. Supposedly, she was less acutely ill than my other inpatients. Intuitively, however, I knew she was very sick and something bad was going to happen to her; I just didn't know what.

Around three o'clock that afternoon, I could no longer

fight my compulsion to put the crash cart outside her room, so I gave in. While no one was looking, I scooted the crash cart down and across the hall just a little bit and placed it beside the door to her room. I checked on my patient, who was sitting up in bed, laughing and talking with a room full of visitors. Then I went back down the hall to the nurses' station. A few moments later, another nurse came walking down the hall towards the nurses' station and wanted to know why the crash cart was at room 201. Everyone seemed to shrug their shoulders with an attitude of indifference and never look up at the inquisitive nurse. Once the hallway was clear, I crept down and returned the crash cart to its rightful place. When four o'clock rolled around, I called the doctor to see if he might be able to come upstairs soon to discharge my patient. His nurse told me he was still in surgery and would be up as soon as he was out. I kept an hourly check on this patient. She always had company and appeared to be doing fine. At six o'clock, the C.N.A. (Certified Nursing Assistant) assigned to this patient rounded on her and found her unresponsive. She was not breathing, and she didn't have a pulse. All her visitors had gone home, and she was alone, so there was no one to ask what had happened. The CNA pulled the code blue cord, and the unit secretary called a code blue to room 201 over the intercom.

My intuition had been spot-on all day, but there was no evidential reason to intervene. The observation patient I had been worried about without knowing why actually needed the crash cart now because she had a pulmonary embolism. Her earlier clinical picture hadn't indicated a problem. Her vital signs had been stable all day. Her respirations were always even and unlabored. The nausea she had earlier that morning subsided. She didn't require narcotic pain medication because her pain was relieved with Tylenol.

I ran and got the crash cart and placed it inside her room this time while the CNA and another R.N. started CPR. I broke the seal off the cart and gave the code team a quick report on this patient when they arrived. They wasted no time and were able to resuscitate her within five minutes. She was transferred to the intensive care unit and discharged home a few days later. Her guardian angel worked hard that day, trying to get me to intervene.

He Called Her Baby

Understandably, I have always tried to avoid giving messages while on duty at my nursing job. Not all spirits, however, have shared my agenda. Some spirits persisted until they got their message through to the intended party. On this particular day, I was working on the orthopedic unit and was assigned a patient who had an ORIF (open reduction and internal fixation) of the right femur a few days earlier and was sitting in her wheelchair for the first time since her surgery. She had requested pain medication, so I went down to her room to administer it. I was standing by her right side when I perceived an intense, icy chill up and down the left side of my body. I searched around for any air conditioning vents that could have blown a blast of icy cold air on me, but there were none. The cold lingered and affected only my left side. The right side of my body felt warm and normal. It was then that I realized an astral entity was invading my space. I telepathically said to this entity:

"I know you're there. Who are you?"

He quickly replied, "I am the husband."

I said, "Okay. What do you want?"

He said, "I need to give her a message."

I asked him, "Don't you see my closed sign? I am at work, and I can't give your message."

He responded, "Please, you have to. It's a matter of life and death! I will not leave you alone until you give her my message!"

I told him again, "I can't give your message. It might jeopardize my job! I need my job!"

That's when he said to me, "We won't let anything happen to your job."

I quickly responded, "What is this 'we' business?"

He said, "We are the people on this side who love her and are concerned for her wellbeing. She will die before her time if you don't give her the message."

> I relented and agreed to give the message, trusting that nothing would happen to my job. I asked this spirit to give me validation of his identity as her husband.
>
> He said, "Tell her that I called her 'Baby' and she called me 'Daddy'."

I prefaced the message to my patient by telling her, "I have a man in spirit with me who says he's your husband and that he called you 'Baby' and you called him 'Daddy'." He's also telling me he died from a chronic illness that caused him to waste away. I asked her if she wanted to hear the message.

She burst into tears and said, "Yes, of course I do. I lost my husband about six months ago, and I miss him so much. He called me 'Baby, and I called him 'Daddy.' He died from AIDS. How could you know?"

I told her, "I know because I have abilities and your husband is standing beside me."

While pointing to her T-shirt, she said, "See this T-shirt. It's a picture of my dead husband. I haven't worn this T-shirt in several months. Why would I be compelled to have my friend bring it to the hospital so I could wear it today?"

I told her, "Maybe it's your husband's way of letting you know that he is with you."

I had not noticed the t-shirt up to this point because I was standing beside her. She was also wearing a patient gown over her tee shirt and fleece shorts, which partially covered the tee shirt. The message from her husband continued as follows:

> *You need to stop hanging out with the crowd you've been seeing because they are leading you down a destructive path of drugs and alcohol. If you don't, something bad will happen to you very soon. Go back to New York and live with your mother. I know that I wasn't always on the right path, and I didn't always go to church, but I'm glad we started going before I died. Please attend church with your mother and make new friends there. I love you and will be with you. I want you to have a full life and find true love again.*

At this point, my patient was sobbing. With tears streaming down her face, she said:

> *Everything he's saying is true. My mom has been telling me that I need to go home to New York and start going to church with her because the people I'm hanging with are into drugs. I know something bad is going to happen to me if I don't get away from them and get some help. It's just so hard, and I miss my husband so much. I can't make it alone! I talked to my mother yesterday, and she will be here in a few days to pick me up when I get discharged from the hospital. I'm returning to New York with her.*

I wasn't on duty when Baby was discharged. I hope she went through with her plan to go home with her mother to New York and get her life together. I also hope that she has achieved the healthy and happy life that she deserves.

Helen, The Dead But Dedicated Nurse

I was sitting at the medical-surgical nurses' station performing chart audits when nurse Helen first appeared to me. She had ash-blonde hair, blue-green eyes, thin lips, a narrow bridged nose, and an oval-shaped face. Nurse Helen was not working that day. She had not worked for several decades because she was dead. Helen was on a mission to get a message to her husband, who would be visiting a friend at the hospital later that day. After making her presence known, she said to me in a stern voice, "Pay attention to me, and please write down my message. He will be here this afternoon, and you must give him the note." So I took out a blank nurse's progress note from the desk drawer and began to write as she dictated the following message:

> *Tell him I am so grateful he was my husband in life. I want to thank him for taking such good care of me while I was sick. I know he still loves me, and I love him, but he's been alone for too long. Tell him it's okay to marry the new lady he's been dating. She will make him very happy. I am moving on to a higher place now. I will no longer be with him in spirit. I release him for all eternity as my husband. I want a divorce. Tell him to let go of me so I can move on.*

It was about 10:30 a.m. when Helen made her appearance before me, and I recorded her message. When 1:00 p.m. arrived, I joined several of my administrative cohorts at a nearby popular Mexican restaurant, where we frequently met for lunch. We had the usual fare, whatever the daily special was, and the usual conversations about family, vacations, special events, and work issues. The waitresses who worked at this restaurant took very good care of us as a group. They always took our orders promptly and served our food quickly because they knew we needed to get back to work on time. I didn't participate in the conversation as much as I normally would because my thoughts kept returning to Nurse Helen and the message she wanted me to give to her husband.

On the drive back to the hospital, I thought about returning to my office to work on crunching some numbers and doing some statistical analysis for the upcoming Clinical Quality Control meeting scheduled later that week. As soon as I thought of returning to my office, however, Nurse Helen quickly and adamantly chimed in my ear:

> *You have to go back to the nurses' station. You have to work there so you can give my husband the message I gave you. He will be there soon. You can get back to your office after that if you want to!*

I pulled into my assigned parking space and walked back over to the main hospital, which was on the other side of the small parking lot. The med/surg unit seemed unusually calm as I walked down the hallway toward the nurses' station. The secretary was sitting in her usual chair at the front counter when I arrived. There were plenty of places for me to sit and audit charts. Nurse Helen chimed in once again and told me that I needed to sit behind the secretary, close to the counter facing the hallway. After I had audited several charts, I glanced up at the clock and noticed it was already 4 p.m. I thought to myself, If he doesn't come within the next 15 minutes, I'm going back to my office. No sooner than I had that thought, Helen broke through and said, "Just wait, he's on the way now. He should be here in about five minutes." I sat there and periodically glanced up at the clock.

Sure enough, five minutes later, Helen's husband came strolling up to the nurses' station and introduced himself to the secretary. He said he wanted to stop by for old times' sake. He began talking about his dead wife, who had passed away three decades earlier. They both worked at the hospital before she became ill. He worked days as a maintenance man, and she worked evenings as a medical-surgical nurse. He would stop by the nurse's station every day and have dinner with her when he got off work before going home. Of course, my ears perked up, and I listened as he continued to talk to the secretary about his deceased wife. He said she won an award one year for being the most dedicated nurse at the hospital. Every year, the hospital would give an award in recognition of their most dedicated nurse.

He said, "See that plaque hanging on the wall right there?"

He pointed to the back wall in the doctor's charting room behind me.

"That was her award."

I turned around to look, and sure enough, a wooden plaque hanging on the wall had the name *Helen Jones* on it. I had never taken notice of it before. At that point, I stood up, walked over to the counter, and introduced myself. I told him I needed to speak with him briefly and indicated we should move down the hallway, away from the nurse's station. We walked to the end of the hallway and stood over to one side. I pulled the note out of my lab jacket, unfolded it, and handed it to him. I told him I depended on my job for income and that giving messages on the job was rare. I asked him to please keep this interaction between us a secret because no one at work knew about this aspect of me.

He cocked his head to the side and looked at me with an expression of bewilderment. He didn't say anything to me but started reading the note. A few moments later, he looked up at me with a tear-stained face and exclaimed:

Oh my God! There's this lady that I have been seeing for the last few years, and I want to marry her, but I feel as if I would betray my dead wife if I did. Thank you for giving me this message. I know it's really okay to move on now. Don't worry, I won't tell anybody about our conversation, but please don't avoid your gift.

After my conversation with Mr. Jones, I walked back towards the nurses' station, wondering how I was supposed to use this gift. At that time, there were no television mediums, and it never occurred to me that some people make a career out of giving these kinds of messages professionally. They're called mediums.

~ Five ~

HOSPITAL HAUNTS

Death is no more than passing from one room into another.
—Helen Keller

The Ghost Who Couldn't Find Her Baby!

I was not hired to work the night shift at this small, rural hospital, which I'll refer to as *Jay County General*; however, because of the nursing shortage we were experiencing for the night shift, all the nurses on the orthopedic and mother-baby units were required to rotate days and nights every two weeks. I was assigned to alternate between these two units on each six-week schedule while rotating shifts. Working the night shift definitely did not agree with my own circadian rhythm. I never liked working nights because it was such a struggle for me. I had a very hard time sleeping during the day, even with blackout curtains in my bedroom. If the sun was up, my body automatically knew it and would say to me, *Get up! The sun is shining outside. You're supposed to be awake.* At night, the cessation of the hustle and bustle of daily activities created by diagnostic and surgical services faded into a deathly silence that permeated every nook and cranny of the nursing unit. For a psychic medium, the dead calm that settles over a hospital nursing unit when the lights are dimmed and the patients are sleeping is very conducive to receiving spirit communication. Add to this the hotbed of spiritual activity in an old hospital, and you have the perfect combination for continual bombardment by spirit entities. Most of the entities that contacted me at work were restless souls trying to resolve unfinished business. These souls were trapped in the astral plane and needed help crossing over. While working at this hospital, I encountered many of these "lost souls." One such soul was a woman named Maddie.

I met Maddie about two o'clock in the morning as I walked down the mother-baby hall on the way to a patient's room. I was about halfway down the hall when I saw the spirit of a young woman coming out of a patient's room about two doors down from me on the left. As I looked a little closer, I noticed that she was floating in midair. She had her hands over her eyes and appeared to be sobbing. She was wearing an old-fashioned-looking white cotton hospital gown. At first sight, this ghost looked so solid that I thought she was a living person. This impression lasted only a few seconds before I realized that she was floating in mid-air. I asked her for her name.

She stopped crying, looked up at me, and said, "My name is Madeline, but they call me Maddie. Somebody took my baby, and I don't know where he is. Can you help me find him?"

As she was speaking, she moved closer and stopped about three feet in front of me. From this distance, I could see that she had light brown hair, which was long and disheveled; her face was oval; her nose was long and narrow; her lips were thin; and she had blue eyes. She looked to be about five feet tall and slender.

I said I was sorry, but I hadn't seen her baby. I told her she needed to come with me to an empty room so we could talk without being disturbed. She followed me into the next room on my left, which was empty. I asked her what she remembered about her baby.

She replied, "The nurse took my baby away while I was in bed. I could hear him crying, but I couldn't move or get out of bed to get to him, and I haven't seen him since. I have looked everywhere, and I can't find him."

While listening to her story, it occurred to me that Maddie could have died from any number of antepartum or postpartum complications, such as:

- Placenta Previa, which blocks the baby's exit from the vaginal canal, is a life-threatening condition for mother and baby.
- Abruptio Placentae, which is a premature separation of the placenta from the uterus, is a life-threatening condition for mother and baby.
- Peripartum and postpartum hemorrhage caused

many women to bleed to death during childbirth in Maddie's time.
- Puerperal Fever—which in the days before antibiotics was a common cause of postpartum mortality for the mother.
- Preeclampsia—a serious blood pressure condition—is life-threatening, especially for the mother, and can occur during pregnancy or after giving birth.
- Milk leg—a condition in which blood clots in the legs can travel to the heart or lungs, resulting in the death of the mother.
- Amniotic embolism, which occurs when the fluid surrounding the baby makes its way into the mother's blood circulation during or shortly after labor, resulting in the death of the mother.

I asked Maddie if she could remember what was happening to her before they took her baby away.

She said, "I think I felt light-headed, and they said there was a lot of blood everywhere. I remember them rubbing my belly, and it started to hurt really bad. That's all I remember. What did they do with my baby?"

I replied, "Maddie, I think they had to hold your baby for you because you needed help with your womb, which is the part of your body that contained and nurtured your baby while he was inside of you. After the doctor delivered your baby, your womb was soft and boggy and failed to contract enough to slow down the bleeding. That's why they rubbed your belly, hoping that it would cause your womb to firm up and slow down the blood flow. Maddie, it sounds like you may have passed away because you lost too much blood."

She said, "What are you talking about? If I were dead, I would be in heaven with Jesus. I wouldn't be here looking for my baby!"

I told her that her need to find her baby in the earthly realm was probably keeping her from crossing over into heaven and that she would be able to reunite with her baby when she crossed over into the light, where she would also be with Jesus and God.

She looked puzzled for a moment and asked, "Am I really dead?"

I told her, "Yes, Honey, you have passed out of your physical body and are in your astral body. You can go be with Jesus in the light and be reunited with your baby, who may be all grown up by now, but he is still your baby."

I created a portal by visualizing an arched doorway with the light of Heaven shining through it, and I told her that she could walk through it and be reunited with her baby and other loved ones that had already crossed over. She stepped one foot over the threshold of the portal and turned around to look at me. I looked at her reassuringly and told her that it was okay; she could go on.

I heard her exclaim, "I see my baby; he's all grown up, and he's with my mother, father, and my grandchildren. Thank you! I will see you again one day and introduce you to my family!"

Then Maddie disappeared from my sight, and the portal closed.

The Sundowning Spirit

Not long after I started my new job as Clinical Quality Director at E. H. Hospital, I encountered the Sundowner. I was walking towards the rear entrance of the hospital late one winter afternoon as the sun was setting, casting its warm, orange glow on the floor and walls of the corridor, when I encountered the spirit of a short, thin elderly man dressed in a light blue hospital gown. He floated in front of me once from my left to my right and then started to pace along my left side as I continued to walk.

He began shouting, "Help! Help! Help!"

When I asked him why he was shouting, "Help," he replied, "I'm lost, and I don't know where my wife is. The nurses won't let me go home. They say I'm confused and I have to stay here. They even tie me down at night."

As I stopped and looked around, I realized that the locked door to my left led to the psychiatric unit. This was the only door that connected the psychiatric unit to the rest of the hospital. While standing there, it occurred to me that this spirit had been a psychiatric patient on the unit when he passed away and never realized he had died. His belief that he was physically restrained by the hospital nursing staff kept him from seeing the light and crossing over.

I asked this spirit if he knew he had passed away and that he no longer had a physical body.

He replied, "What are you talking about?"

I told him he no longer had a physical body and that he could go to heaven if he wanted to.

He stopped pacing, looked straight at me, and said, "Lady, you're the one who's crazy. I have a body. I can see my body. I know I have a body. I'm not that crazy."

I thought to myself, *Well, I was right about him coming from the psychiatric unit.*

He went on to say, "Look, Lady, I just want to go home to my wife. Can you help me do that?"

I asked him if he saw a light or a tunnel with a light at the end of it.

He replied, "No."

I told him that if he listened to me and did exactly as I said, I could help him go home.

He happily agreed and said, "Okay, but please hurry up!"

In my mind, I created an opening to a heavenly paradise at the far end of the hallway. I called upon the Holy Angels and loved ones in Spirit to come and greet this lost soul at the entrance to the light and to escort him to the level of heaven where paradise exists. I also asked them to reconnect him with his wife at some point in time. I then told this lost soul that for him to be discharged and sent home where he could be with his wife, he would have to come with me to the big light at the end of the hall so that the discharge attendants could take him home. He said, "Okay, let's go!"

So, I turned and walked back down the hall in the opposite direction from where I was originally headed. I asked him if he could see the attendants standing just inside the bright light. He said, "Yes. How come they have so many lights on?" I told him they had a lot of lights on because they needed to be able to see which way to go to take people home from the hospital.

When we reached the end of the hall, I said goodbye and watched as this rescued soul stepped into the entrance of the Light and was quickly carried away by angels and his loved ones in Spirit. He never looked back. I watched as the Light got smaller and smaller and was no longer visible. Once the light completely disappeared, I continued to walk through the front entrance of the hospital. I decided to go to my office, get my purse, and call it a day. I was feeling a little drained; I had definitely gone beyond the call of duty that day and was ready to go to my own home!

The Ghost Of Nurse Abigail Is Still Working

I first encountered Nurse Abigail in the back hall of the med-surg unit at about three o'clock in the morning. I volunteered to work as a staff nurse on the floor while we were in the process of closing down the hospital. Many staff nurses resigned upon hearing the news release that we were not going to be able to build a new hospital because we were denied the Certificate of Need from the state to do so. We were not going to be able to keep our doors open for very much longer because the building that housed our hospital was considered to be functionally obsolete and unsafe. According to certain regulatory authorities, our hallways were too narrow to handle an emergency evacuation situation, and to top that off, we didn't even have a sprinkler system. To continue as a hospital, we needed a new facility. We had the financing, but we didn't have a new state-issued Certificate of Need, which initially we were told we wouldn't need until we formed a partnership with another hospital. The certificate that we needed went to build a new government-funded county hospital in a nearby town. We were a private hospital, so, of course, we were passed over.

As I stated earlier, it was three o'clock in the morning, and I had just purchased a can of Diet Mountain Dew from the vending machine in the surgical waiting room. When I walked out and back into the hall, I saw the ghost of Nurse Abigail stick her head out of an empty patient room. I blinked my eyes several times and wondered if I might be sleepwalking. I told myself to wake up, but I still saw her as she walked out of that room and proceeded slowly down the hall, peeking into each room as she went. I took a sip of my Mountain Dew and concluded that I was very much awake. When I passed Abigail, she noticed me, quickly turned around, and came toward me. I thought to myself, *Oh no, she sees me.* As Abigail came closer, I noticed she was wearing a light blue, long-sleeved cotton dress that hung down to her ankles. This dress was covered with a white pinafore apron that was the same length as her dress. On her feet, she wore black lace-up shoes with a two-inch heel. Wrapped around her head was a white cotton scarf that tied at the nape of her neck.

Looking straight at me, she said, "You can see me, can't you?"

I replied, Yes, I can."

I asked her what her name was, and she said, "My name is Abigail, and I am a nurse here at this Hospital."

I said, "Okay. What year is it?"

She replied, "It's 1918, and you sure are dressed funny. What and who are you? Are you from the future? Don't tell anybody, but sometimes I see things in the future. Are you one of my visions?"

I replied to her that I was also a nurse and that the current year was 2003. I said it sounded like she had a gift from God known as precognition while she was alive, which meant that she was able to perceive events that would happen in the future. I told her that I had abilities too, but mine included being able to see spirits. I asked her if she remembered passing away.

She said, "No, I don't remember dying. I know I was very sick while I continued to care for my patients with influenza. I haven't seen any angels or anybody I know. I think I may have died from the Gripp (Spanish Influenza Epidemic of 1919), but if I died, shouldn't I be in heaven?"

I told her that normally that's what happens, but sometimes we get so caught up in our work that we become attached to it and can't let go of the earth's plane. I also told her that if she wanted me to, I could call the angels, and they would take her to heaven.

She replied, "What if I'm not good enough to go to heaven?"

I said, "God is gracious, and anyone who wants to go to heaven can. God does not judge us—we judge ourselves. God loves and accepts everyone who desires grace."

She said, "Okay, I guess I can trust you."

In my mind, I called out to the Holy Angels and her loved ones in Spirit to take this sweet soul to God in Heaven. I asked them to let her feel God's love and acceptance before they crossed her over so that she would know without any doubts that she was on her way to heaven, not hell. No sooner had I mentally uttered this prayer, than she was surrounded by a bluish-white light and several beautiful angels dressed in silver robes with gold sashes who escorted her up a winding, pearlescent staircase. She glanced back at me, and I heard her say, "Thank you." I told her that she was very welcome and that it was my pleasure to help a fellow nurse in need.

Some Spirits Come And Go As They Please!

My office at E.H. Hospital was located within a cottage-style house situated on the corner of the hospital property. This house had been purchased by the hospital in the 1980s and was being used as administrative office space to free up space within the hospital for clinical use. Constructed in 1909, the house was originally built to provide housing for employees of the Denim Mill located in the center of this small, rural town.

One day around noon, as I walked down the hallway towards the front door of this house, the apparition of an elderly lady with short, white, curly hair appeared beside the front door. She was sweeping the floor with what looked like an old-fashioned broom made of bundled straw tied with twine around a long, round wooden stick with a smooth finish. She glanced up at me and smiled as she continued sweeping. As I took a few steps closer, she stopped and nodded her head as if to gesture to me that it was okay for me to pass by her. She started to fade away as I excused myself and passed by her. Then I realized I was seeing and talking to a ghost. The apparition of this lady was so solid that I initially thought I was seeing a physical person. I saw her again about a week later in the employee kitchen. She was bent over the stove as if she were cooking. The stove was located on the far side of the kitchen, across from the entrance to the dining room, where I was standing. She looked up at me, smiled, and then returned to the task at hand. I mentally asked her who she was. Without looking at me, she replied:

> *My name is Mrs. Jones. My husband and I have lived here for over fifty years. We raised our five children in this house." I asked her if she knew she had passed away and was in a spirit body. She replied, "Yes, My Dear, I know I'm dead. That is, my physical body is dead, but I am very much alive. I like to visit my earthly home once in a while to remember the wonderful life I had here. This house holds so many wonderful memories for me. You don't have to get rid of me like you did with the last two ghosts at the hospital. I know how to come and go all by myself.*

After her last comment, she disappeared from my sight completely. I could hear her say, as her voice gradually faded away, "Goodbye, and God bless. I will visit again soon. Be sure to enjoy your life." I realized Mrs. Jones was a highly evolved, sweet spirit who knew how to use portals to enter and exit the physical world at will. Some spirits can come and go as they please!

~ Six ~

DINING OUT WITH THE SPIRITS

Some people go to mediums to bring them into contact with the spirit world, but most go to bartenders.
~ Evan Esar, 20,000 Quips & Quotes

Some Spirits Have Your Back!

Spirits especially like to interrupt me while I'm dining at restaurants. I have had so many interruptions from Spirit while eating out, you would think I should be skinny by now. One such interruption occurred at a small-town family diner where I ate frequently. The owners had recently hired a new waitress named Anne, who was my waitress on this particular evening. Anne walked over to my table and pleasantly introduced herself. She took my order, and as she walked away from the table, I noticed that there was a spirit attached to her back. This spirit was a very petite elderly lady. She had short, wispy gray hair with a few strands of black hair scattered throughout. Her skin was very wrinkled and light brown with a yellow tinge. As I watched her for a while, the word Lumbee Indian came to me. I asked this spirit who she was and why she was on Anne's back.

She replied, "I'm her grandmother, and I have her back. Tell my granddaughter not to go back to that abusive man she just broke up with. If she stays with him, he's going to hurt her again or possibly kill her."

When Anne came back to the table with my food, I gave her a description of the spirit that I saw on her back, which she immediately validated by saying:

"That's my grandma you just described. She was Lumbee Indian."

After she had validated the description of her grandmother, I told her what her grandmother had said to me about having her back, along with the warning not to go back to the abusive man she just left. Anne replied:

Yep, that's my grandma! She was always on my back about something. I would tell her to get off my back, and she would say that I better be glad she had my back so nothing bad would happen to me. The man she's talking about just called me yesterday and asked me to come back to him. I left him because he was physically abusive. During our last fight, he gave me a black eye and broke my arm. I'm having a hard time trying to make it financially on my own, and I'm very tempted to go back. He really is a good man, and I believe he loves me. I don't know what I'm going to do.

I reminded Anne of what her grandmother had said: that this man would hurt her again or even possibly kill her if she went back. I implored her to please heed her grandmother's warning. I encouraged her not to give up on her independence because the right man would come along soon and he would treat her like a queen. That was the last time I saw Anne. On my next visit to the diner, I was told Anne had quit her job. I hope Anne heeded her grandmother's warning, but I feel she didn't.

Old Mr. Cooley Still Runs The Diner From The Astral Realm

The same small-town diner I talked about in the last story has more than one ghost and an owner. There was a former owner named Mr. Cooley, who is now a ghost. Mr. Cooley was the proprietor of the original restaurant in the 1920s. The restaurant he owned was a much smaller version of the current one. The current owners have made additions to the original structure over the years to provide more dining room areas and a larger kitchen. I happened to be sitting in the original part of the restaurant this particular evening when the spirit of Mr. Cooley made his appearance and introduced himself to me. He was a short, stout, bald man with a rotund belly and a jolly disposition. He wore a blue and white pinstriped suit and a gold pocket watch tucked away in the pocket of his vest. Mr. Cooley started the conversation by thanking me for eating at his establishment and asking me if I liked the food. I told him that the food was delicious as usual and that I enjoyed eating at this restaurant. I asked him if he was aware that he had passed away and that new owners were running the business. He chuckled and said the following:

I know I'm dead, but I still think of the restaurant as my establishment. I sold this place before I passed away. I knew I was getting too old to run the business like it should be run, so I sold it. The people I sold it to sold it to the current owners. When the current owners first bought the place, they did a lot of good things and increased business. They even added a dining area and expanded the kitchen, but over the last several years things have gotten really bad, and they have not taken appropriate measures to try and save the restaurant. I would like for you to give Dawn a message for me because I care a great deal about them and this restaurant. I want Dawn to know that her parents are going to go through some profound changes soon, which will impact the business. Instead of being dictated to by her parents, the owners of the restaurant, Dawn is going to have to step up and take a leadership role. Within a year, her father is going to pass away from a dementia-related illness, and her mother is going to have several surgeries on her joints. Her heart is also failing, and she will not be able to stand the stress of running the business. Her need to be bossy and maintain control is only going to make her heart worse, and she will eventually have a heart attack. Even after Dawn takes on the task of running the business, her mother is going to try to continue to control things and dictate her commands from home. Tell Dawn to do what she needs to do in the best interest of the restaurant and not to bend to her mother's will. Dawn has great ideas for the restaurant that her mother does not approve of. The changes that Dawn believes need to be implemented will make the restaurant successful again and keep it a going concern. Her mother will try to give her much resistance to the changes that need to be made. As I see it, soon her mother will no longer be fit to run the restaurant.

I finished my dinner and headed up front to the cash register to pay for my meal. There was no one in front of or behind me as I approached the counter where Dawn was sitting. Dawn normally worked the evening shift as manager and cashier, and her mother or another employee would fill her role on the day shift. I paid my bill and started small talk about the local upcoming events for the holiday season, hoping that our conversation would lead to the delivery of my message from Mr. Cooley. Dawn was somewhat aware of my abilities from prior conversations. There have been many occasions when we just stood at the counter and talked for five to ten minutes at a time, especially when business was slow, as it was on this particular evening. I finally got up enough nerve to tell her that the original owner of the restaurant introduced himself to me while I was eating. I gave her a description of him, and she verified that he was indeed the original owner. I told her that he had given me a message for her, and I asked her if she wanted to hear it. She told me to follow her into the front dining area, where she pointed to a picture of Mr. Cooley hanging on the wall.

This picture was the exact image of the man I saw in the pinstriped suit. The walls of this restaurant were filled with pictures of faces that were totally unfamiliar to me. I had no idea who all these people were. Many restaurants, like Cracker Barrel, for example, cover their walls with pictures of people from long ago. This restaurant was no different. I followed her back to the cash register, where we continued our conversation. With a quizzical look on her face, Dawn asked me what dear old Mr. Cooley had to say. I gave her the message Mr. Cooley had given me.

Once the message was delivered, Dawn exclaimed, "Oh my God! My father has Alzheimer's disease and is not doing well. We had to put him in a nursing home. My mother was told today by the orthopedic doctor that she needs to have bilateral knee replacements. She was also recently diagnosed with Congestive Heart Failure. As long as she's alive, my mother is not going to let me take charge of the restaurant. I know we have got to start making some effective changes or we're going to go out of business. We've been losing a lot of money. Did Mr. Cooley happen to say anything about my love life?" I chuckled and told her that, unfortunately, Mr. Cooley was quiet on that issue. She asked if she could call me in the future to see if Mr. Cooley had any more messages for her about the restaurant. I told her she could call me anytime she felt like she needed to talk.

The Big Easy Diner Has Spirits

We had never dined at The Big Easy Diner; however, on this particular Sunday afternoon after church, my husband and I felt compelled to try something new for lunch, so we headed downtown, where we discovered this charming and unique diner. We were attracted by the curb appeal of the restaurant and decided to take a chance at it. As soon as we walked in, I perceived spirits everywhere. We were immediately seated at a table in the center of this large restaurant. Within a few minutes of being seated, our waitress appeared with ice water and bread and pleasantly introduced herself. She said she would return in a few minutes after we had decided what we wanted to order. As I sat there looking at the menu, I was constantly distracted by another waitress who frequently walked past our table. I watched as she worked at a frantic pace, trying to appease her customers. As I watched, I began to receive impressions about her troubled life. My impressions were interrupted when our waitress showed up at our table to take our order. After she had taken the order and disappeared out of sight, my impressions returned. An elderly lady with short, white hair and blue eyes appeared to me. She asked me to please tell her granddaughter that things would get better soon and that law school would be a good choice for her.

As soon as we finished lunch, I waved the frantic waitress over to our table. She quickly walked over and asked how she could help us. I told her we didn't need any help but that I had a message for her if she wanted to hear it.

I explained that I was a Psychic medium, and a spirit who said it was her grandmother appeared to me and asked me to give her a message.

She glanced down at me with a quizzical look on her face and said, "Okay, you can tell me."

I started by telling her that as she walked back and forth, passing our table on her way to take care of her customers, I had feelings of restlessness, indecisiveness, and worry that I perceived were coming from her. I then described the spirit that I saw, which she validated as being her grandmother on her mother's side. I told her what the grandmother had said to me—that things would get better soon and law school would be a good choice for her. Once I had given her the message, she put her hands to her mouth and said:

Oh my God. I can't believe this. I recently got divorced and moved to North Carolina from New York with plans to go to school. I want to become a lawyer, but that would take too much time. I had also thought about going to beauty school. It wouldn't take as long, but that's not what I really want to do.

I informed this waitress that it was possible for her to go to school to become a paralegal and obtain her undergraduate degree at the same time. Then she could go on to law school. That way, she could earn some money and gain experience in the legal field. Taking this approach would give her some stability and meet her financial needs while keeping her bigger dream a potential reality.

I told her I felt "lawyer energy" all around her, and I thought Spirit was trying to validate for her that going to law school would be something she could eventually accomplish if she were to set her goals and take things one step at a time.

He's Still Not Good Enough For You!

My husband, Joe, and I were having drinks with three other couples in the bar area of a nice restaurant while we waited to be seated at our table. As we sat there talking and drinking our cocktails, an attractive, middle-aged Indian couple dressed in beautiful, traditional Hindu clothing walked into the bar area. Like most people, my eyes are drawn to activity, and I glanced over at them as they entered the room. Immediately, I heard:

"You know, she could have done a lot better!"

I replied to the voice resonating in my head that she looked as if she was doing pretty well to me.

This spirit replied, "No, she could have married a lot better."

I said, "Okay, who are you, and what do you want?"

She replied, "I'm like her mother."

I asked her what it was that she wanted to convey.

She said, "Just tell her that she could have married a lot better. He's still not good enough for her!"

I told her that I absolutely would not give such a message.

> She said, "Then I won't leave you alone until you do."
>
> I relented and said, "All right, if she is still here when my dinner party has dispersed, I'll give her the message."

A few minutes later, the hostess came into the bar area to seat us at our table in the dining room per our scheduled seven p.m. dinner reservation. The eight of us were seated around a huge round table covered with a white linen tablecloth and adorned by a beautiful centerpiece of fragrant, fresh-cut flowers. The table was set with fine silverware and white linen napkins shaped like swans. About ten minutes after we had been seated, the hostess escorted and seated the Indian couple at the table directly behind me. Now, this in and of itself was of no great significance, but the fact that there were so many empty tables scattered throughout the dining room was significant to me. The hostess had been seating people at tables all over the dining room. Why was it that this couple was seated directly behind me and not at an empty table across the room? Once the couple had been seated at their table, I commented to the *mother spirit* that having them sit directly behind me was very convenient. She replied, "Well, I wanted to make it easy for you."

When dinner was over and my party had all made their way to the door, I stepped over to the table behind me and introduced myself. I told them my name and that I was also a resident of the neighborhood. I said I was a Psychic Medium and explained to them what that meant—that I could communicate with the spirits of people who have passed away. I directed my attention to the lady and told her I had a message from a woman in spirit who said that she was like a mother. I asked her if she wanted to hear the message. She nodded her head and said yes. As instructed by the spirit, I gave her the message exactly as I received it. I told her, "You could have married a lot better, and he's still not good enough for you!" As soon as I delivered the message, this lady's husband ran from behind their table and gave me a big hug while exclaiming, "That's my sister-in-law, and that's what she used to always say to us when she was still alive! She was my wife's oldest sister." I questioned him as to why she referred to herself as being like the mother. He replied, "She was like a mother because she raised my wife after their mother died."

They both laughed and commented on how, even in death, she was as humorous as she was in life. They were very appreciative and gave me many thanks. This gentleman gave me his very ornate business card. He told me his name was Andy, and he was a retired psychiatrist. He said to me, "I think you have a wonderful gift, and I respect you for using it. Keep it up!" I guess I passed the litmus test for good mental health after all. I suppose there are more people than I realize—even psychiatrists—who think psychic mediums are a normal breed. Whatever normal means!

Mother's Day Celebration With The Spirit Of Grandma Sealy

My husband, Michael, and I, along with my daughter, her boyfriend, and her two children, celebrated Mother's Day 2014 by attending church. After church, we continued the celebration by dining at my daughter's favorite Italian Restaurant for lunch. This restaurant was extremely popular; even with a reservation made the day before, we had to wait at least twenty minutes beyond our reservation time to get seated at our table. Once we were seated and had all received our food, I said the blessing, which included an invitation for my mother and grandmother, who were both in spirit, to be with us. Apparently, my mother and grandmother weren't the only spirits present at our Mother's Day lunch that day. There were other mothers and grandmothers present as well. Afterward, when I thought about it, for each mother and grandmother that were physically present, there could easily have been a permutation of at least three spirits with them. One mother and two grandmothers in spirit for each mother and grandmother physically present

Within a couple of minutes after I said the blessing, the spirit of a mature female showed herself to me. She was a short, small-framed lady and was wearing a floral cotton dress that hung down to the calves of her legs. Her dress was covered by a solid-colored pinafore apron. She wore old-fashioned, thick, beige-colored stockings and black lace-up shoes with one to two-inch heels. Her hair was ash blonde with gray streaks, which she wore pulled back into a bun on top of her head. Her face was round, with a narrow, bridged nose and thin lips. She had a pale complexion with a few strawberry-colored freckles across her nose and cheeks and deep wrinkles around her forehead, eyes, and mouth. She had blue-green eyes and wore small, oval, wire-rimmed glasses. I asked her who she was, and she said:

> "I'm Grandma Sealy."
>
> I said okay and asked her what she wanted.
> She replied, "I would like for you to give a message to my granddaughter."
>
> I asked her who her granddaughter was, and she said, "My granddaughter's name is Sarah. Turn around and look behind you."
>
> I did as she said and turned around to look behind me. Sure enough, sitting at the head of the table behind me was a much younger and more modern version of the woman that had just appeared to me in my vision. She was having Mother's Day lunch with her daughter and three grandchildren.
>
> I asked Grandma Sealy what the message was for her granddaughter.
>
> She replied, "Tell her that I am proud of her and her children and grandchildren, but she needs to go back to church and take her grandchildren with

her so that they can receive a proper religious upbringing."

I told Grandma Sealy that I would go over and give the message after I had finished with my own Mother's Day lunch with the condition that I would also tell her granddaughter, Sarah, that she has the right to make her own decisions and that no one else, not even a sweet grandma spirit, has the right to dictate to her how to live her life or tell her what to do. I went on to say that I appreciated how much she cared for her granddaughter, and I understood that she had only the best intentions for her, but that we all have the right to make our own decisions.

Her only reply to me was, "Be sure to let her know that I love her to the moon and back."

Once my Mother's Day lunch was over and my family headed for the door, I stepped over to the table behind me and delivered the message to Grandma Sealy's granddaughter, Sarah, just as I promised I would do. As usual, I started the message by introducing myself and asking for permission to give it.

After describing Grandma Sealy's physical appearance, Sarah looked up at me and smiled. With tears gently flowing down her face, she said, "Please tell me everything my Grandma Sealy said."

I gave her the message that her grandma had given

me about going to church, with the caveat that no spirit, not even a sweet grandma spirit, has the right to tell you what to do. I told her that it was important that we make our own decisions in life and that all our decisions should come from within us, not from an external source, even if they appear right.

Sarah said, "I have been thinking about it a lot here lately. I know that I need to start going to church again, and I should take my grandchildren with me."

Sarah burst out sobbing when I told her that her grandma Sealy said that she loved her to the moon and back.

Her reply to me was, "We always said that to each other. That's the last thing I said to her before she died." She then said to her grandma, "Grandma Sealy, I love you to the moon and back too!"

It wasn't until after I had delivered the message that I noticed my grandson had not left with the rest of the family but stayed by my side. He stood about two feet behind me and paid attention to everything I had to say to Mrs. Sealy's granddaughter. As we walked away from the table, My grandson asked me, "Nonna, how did you do that? Can you teach me how?"

I told him if he had the ability and wanted to be a Medium one day, I would gladly share with him how to do the work.

He smiled, gave me a big hug, and said, "I love you, Nonna!"

~ Seven ~

THE SPIRITS ARE ALWAYS OUT & ABOUT

You think the dead we loved truly ever leave us? You think that we don't recall them more clearly in times of great trouble?

— J.K. Rowling, Harry Potter and the Prisoner of Azkaban

At The Dentist's Office

Unfortunately, I fractured a tooth while eating almonds and had to have a crown placed to repair the damage. As I lay there in the dentist's chair with my mouth full of dental implements, the spirit of the dental assistant's grandmother bombarded me incessantly about how smart her granddaughter was and that she should be the dentist and not the dental assistant.

She stated, "I need you to tell my granddaughter that

she is too smart to be working as a dental assistant, and it is beneath her. Tell her she needs to go to dental school so she can have a real profession that pays well. She is wasting precious time, which she can't get back."

I told this spirit there was no way I would give such a message because, as individuals, we have the right to make our own decisions. No one else has the right to dictate to us, not even well-intentioned grandmothers. I also told her that I was a grandmother too, and I understood how much she cared for her granddaughter. As grandmothers, we need to let our granddaughters make their own decisions.

Her reply to me was, "I will not leave you alone in peace until you tell her what I said."

I said okay, but with one condition: I also told her that she has the right to make her own choices and that she should always listen to her own inner voice.

I asked this grandma spirit to give me evidential information I could give to her granddaughter. She showed herself to have blonde hair, blue eyes, an aquiline nose, thin lips, and a pale oval face. She was slender, about 5'7" tall, and dressed in fine clothing. She made it clear to me that she definitely belonged to the upper class in her earthly life. Next, I saw her standing in a large, luxurious, wood-paneled room lined with bookshelves brimming with books. This room was filled with beautiful, stately furnishings such as mahogany desks, leather sofas, and wingback chairs. Apparently, it was the study of her home and reeked of aristocracy. She gave me a tour of the rest of her huge home and told me she came from old money.

Next, she showed me a scene where she was playing bridge with friends and told me she was also a member of the yacht club.

It seemed as if an hour passed before my mouth was finally free to speak. As soon as the dentist left the treatment room, I conjured up the nerve to convey the message. I opened up the communication by telling Carla I was a Psychic Medium, which meant that I could communicate with the souls of people who had passed away. I told her I had a spirit with me who said it was her grandmother. I gave her the above-noted description as evidence of her communication with me.

Carla immediately responded to my description by saying, "Yep, that's what my grandmother looked like; she had blonde hair, blue eyes, and was tall and slender. She was a socialite. She played bridge and belonged to the Yacht Club. She had lots of money."

I asked her if she wanted to hear the message.

After pausing for a few seconds, she said, "Sure, I can already imagine what she has to say to me."

I prefaced the message by saying we all have the right to make our own decisions and that all of our decisions should come from within ourselves, not from any spirit or any living person. I proceeded to tell her what her grandmother had told me—that she should be in school to become a dentist and that working as a dental assistant was beneath her. I also told her that her grandmother said there was no time to waste; she needed to go back to school to become a dentist so she could have a real profession that paid well.

Carla replied, "I am not surprised to hear her say that. She always made me feel like I wasn't good enough. You can tell her, I am happy doing what I'm doing, and I am never going back to school."

I told her that her grandmother could hear her and that she could talk directly to her if she wanted to. I also told her I didn't want to give the message, but her grandmother threatened to harass me until I did. I let Carla know that I also have a granddaughter, and I believe my granddaughter has the right to live life as she chooses, so I wasn't in agreement with her grandmother's message. In Carla's defense, I said in an audible voice to her grandmother that granddaughters must be allowed to make their own choices.

At The Massage Parlor

My husband Joe and I were having a couples massage, and I guess I was feeling a little too relaxed because I began to see a vision of a short, stout lady with cropped gray hair. I asked her who she was, and she replied, "I am her grandmother!"

I said, Okay, who's your granddaughter?

She said, "Her name is Judy; she's the one giving you a massage."

I replied, "Okay, what's your message?"

She answered, "Tell my granddaughter not to worry; she will have permanent love."

I lay there face down on the table, feeling apprehensive

about delivering another message in public while on a date with my husband.

After a few minutes of hesitation, I finally decided to tell my young massage therapist that I was a psychic medium and could communicate with souls who had passed away. I told her about the older woman I was seeing and described her features. Judy began to cry, tears covering her cheeks, and told me I had just described her mother's mother. I asked her if she wanted to hear the message. After a few moments of choking on her tears, she said yes, so I delivered the message practically verbatim. I told her that her grandmother said she would have permanent love.

The young massage therapist replied, "That's what she always said about having children—that they will give you permanent love."

I explained to the massage therapist that what her grandmother was trying to say was that she would have permanent romantic love. I told her that her grandmother showed me a man in his mid-thirties who was over six feet tall, about three hundred pounds, with brown eyes, black hair, and a black beard.

After I had described his physical appearance, she said, "He sounds like the guy I have been dating for the last six months. But my grandmother always said that it was children that gave you permanent love, and I have two of them now, a boy and a girl."

I reassured her that when her grandmother showed me the picture of the man she was dating, she made it clear to me that this man would be her permanent love, not her children.

Judy stopped crying and began to smile, saying, "I am so happy to hear this because before I met this man, I really was starting to believe no man would ever want a permanent relationship with me. I've been hoping and praying that this man is different from all the others, but I'm afraid of getting my hopes up. On a deeper level, I really feel like he's the one I will spend my life with."

I told her that her grandma certainly believes he will be the one she spends the rest of her life with because he will give her permanent love!

The Motorcycle Riding Ghost At The DMV

Anyone who has ever had the pleasure of waiting at the Division of Motor Vehicles Office to get a driver's license renewed knows how long and monotonous the wait can be. I took my book along with me that day, hoping I might pass the time more quickly by reading. I purchased the book about a week earlier and wanted to get started on it but had not had the opportunity. Little did I know I wouldn't be getting started on it that day either. As soon as I sat down and opened the book, I started having visions of a young man on a motorcycle driving down a winding country road lined with oak trees with yellow ribbons tied around each one. He was dressed in all black: a black leather jacket, black leather boots, and a black helmet with a face shield. I remember trying to get rid of the vision by gently shaking my head, but that didn't work. Whenever I tried to focus my attention on comprehending the words in my book, the vision popped into my head again and would not leave. I finally gave up and allowed the vision to play out like a movie.

I watched as a man on a red motorcycle rounded the next curve. I noticed a small, white, A-framed house to his right, which was situated on a tract of land about an eighth of a mile away from the paved country road. A huge oak tree stood in the front yard, close to the entrance of the narrow dirt path that led up to the house. I realized that all of the other oak trees in my vision had yellow ribbons tied around them except for this one. As I pondered the meaning of the yellow ribbons, it occurred to me that this spirit was looking for forgiveness and acceptance. I looked up and noticed a moving, empty rocking chair on the front porch. The man on the motorcycle momentarily stopped on the side of the road to take a look at the oak tree in the front yard and resumed driving when he saw that there was no yellow ribbon tied around it. I asked this spirit who he was, and with a strong male voice, he replied:

"My name is 'T'."

I told him that if I was going to relay his message, he would have to give me his full name.

Once again, he replied, "My name is 'T'. Just tell her I said my name is 'T'."

I said, "Okay, what is your message?"

He said, "Tell her I am in a good place and at peace,

but the family needs to forgive me so they can be at peace too."

I asked him to whom he needed me to give the message.

He said, "It's the pretty, young African American girl sitting beside you on your right."

I told him that I would try my best to give her the message. Then, I watched him disappear out of sight as he rode his bike into the blood-orange blazing fire of a setting sun.

After a few moments of gathering enough courage, I turned to my right and introduced myself to the young lady sitting beside me. I gave her my name, told her that I was a psychic medium, and explained to her that I could communicate with people who had passed away. I told her that a spirit named "T" had just communicated with me and wanted me to give her a message. I asked her if she wanted to hear it, and after briefly hesitating, she said yes. "Yes, I want to hear it. 'T' was my cousin, who died about six months ago. He died in a motorcycle accident." I told her he said he was in a good place and at peace, but he needed the family to forgive him. I also told her I watched as he rode his red motorcycle into the setting sun. This young lady burst into tears and said:

Well, he's doing what he's always loved to do—riding

that damn motorcycle. I am so happy for him, but I can't forgive him for what he did to the family, especially my grandmother. The day before he died, he was supposed to visit our grandmother, but he never showed up. She sat in her rocking chair on the front porch of her little country home all day long, waiting for him to come driving up the dirt path on that damn motorcycle, but he never showed up. The next day, when she got the news that he had been killed in a motorcycle accident, she had a heart attack and died. I can't forgive him for that. I want to, but I just can't right now. It will take more time.

"T" chimed in my ear, "Please tell her it's important for the family to forgive me, not for my sake but for their sake, so they can have peace. I am in a good place, and Grandma is with me. We can all be together again."

I heard a sweet little voice say, "Alicia, it was my time to go. I am in heaven, and your cousin is with me. Tell everyone to stop this nonsense. If they want to be forgiven, then they must also forgive. We can all be together again one day."

When I told Alicia what her grandmother had said, she burst into tears again and replied, "I will try to forgive him, but it will take time. I will tell the rest of the family about this, but I can't make them forgive him either."

Alicia thanked me and hugged my neck just before she was called up to the desk. I settled in once again and thought that I might get some reading done. No sooner had I opened my book, I was also called up to the desk. It just wasn't meant for me to accomplish any reading that day—reading books, that is. I seemed to be on a roll reading, people!

In The Church Sanctuary

My husband, Michael, and I had been attending Unity Church for about nine months when a member of the choir approached me after the second Sunday morning service and asked me if I could connect her with a friend of hers who had passed away about twenty years earlier. I told her I couldn't promise he would come through, but I would try. She said his name was Little Joe, and she had thought about him constantly since he died and wanted to know if he was okay. I took a few moments to tune into Spirit and invited "Little Joe" to come forward.

Within a few seconds, a young man in his mid-thirties appeared to me in what looked like a snapshot from the early 1970s. At about five feet nine, he was standing in the middle of what seemed to be a dance floor. Slender with a muscular build, he had short brown hair, hazel eyes, a narrow nose, and thin lips. He was dressed in a button-down blue and white pinstriped cotton shirt, blue jeans, and leather penny loafers. He seemed like a very sweet and free-spirited person. He showed me his lifestyle of partying and having many male lovers. He also showed me scenes where he was dancing and doing drugs with Debbie. He said she was the best friend he had ever had, and she would have been the perfect partner if he hadn't been gay. He made me feel his passing, which happened quickly. He said he really wasn't expecting to die during that particular hospitalization because he had been hospitalized before for treatment with IV antibiotics and antifungals and then discharged home. He made me feel the raging fever, aches, and pains he experienced all over his body as he was dying. I could taste blood in my mouth, and I felt as if I were septic. He told me he had been diagnosed with HIV in the mid 1980s. He showed me several medicine bottles and said he tried to take care of himself once he found out he was infected, but there was no medication at that time to effectively treat HIV/AIDS, and there was nothing anyone could do. He had died from a full-blown AIDS Complex. He told me to tell Debbie not to worry about him; he had made his peace with the Creator while he was dying. He said, "I called out to him, and he responded to me with love and acceptance."

Afterwards, Debbie showed me a picture of Little Joe that she had taken in the early 1970s and uploaded to her cell phone just a few weeks before our reading. He was tall and slender and looked the same as I had seen him in my vision with the button-down shirt, blue jeans, loafers, brown hair, and hazel eyes. When I asked Debbie why she called him Little Joe, she admitted she was trying to fool me. She chuckled and apologized to me when I told her it obviously didn't work.

At The Meat Counter

Shopping for quality meat at a good price can be quite a chore. I tend to have a one-track mind when it comes to shopping, especially for meat. We were having dinner guests that evening, and I wanted to find the best steaks possible for the money. I was definitely on a mission. I usually don't allow myself to become distracted by anything or anybody when I'm shopping; however, Spirit always has its own agenda and doesn't mind interrupting mine.

I found two perfect steaks and had two more to find when Spirit showed me a vision of a woman's left ovary with a large mass on it. When I asked Spirit why I was seeing this vision, I was made aware of the lady standing at the meat counter just a few feet to my right. Four ladies with colorful saris appeared to me clairvoyantly, and the one standing on the far right in my vision said: "I'm her mother, and I'm here with my mother, my grandmother, and my sister. Tell my daughter there's good news. It's going to be okay. She doesn't have cancer."

I looked up and down the meat counter, and there was no one else standing there but me and the lady to my right. I sighed and edged my way over to where she was standing. I finally got up the nerve to strike up a conversation with her and introduce myself. I told her that four women had appeared to me, all wearing colorful saris.

She looked at me as if she were in shock and said, "That has to be my mother, aunt, grandmother, and great-grandmother. They have all passed away now, but they were very close to each other in life. My mother was the last one to pass away. After she died, I left India with my husband and children to start a new life here in the U.S., and I haven't been back since. There's no reason to go back. My husband has a very successful business here in the States, and we are very happy."

I told her I thought that was wonderful.

She continued to talk about her family and then asked me why I saw her ancestors. I took a deep breath and let it out slowly. I told her I had been shown a picture of a lump on an ovary with a message for her not to worry because there would be good news and she would be okay. Tears started to stream down her face, and she gave me a hug.

She said, "I had a biopsy done yesterday, and I'm waiting for the results. I am hoping that it's just a lipoma (a lipoma is a tumor consisting of fatty tissue and is typically benign)."

I told her that no matter what it was, she was going to have a good outcome.

She said, "I can confidently say I know I will be okay now. Thank you, Shirl. Keep doing the good work!"

She walked away with a smile on her face, and I returned to shopping for two more steaks. Somehow, finding the best steaks didn't matter so much anymore.

At The Beauty Shop

It was a beautiful spring day, and I was off duty from the hospital, so I decided to go to the beauty shop and get a long-overdue haircut. I had been preparing for my move to Florida with my new husband, Joe, for the past several weeks, and between working and preparing for the move, I hadn't had any time for myself. I didn't bother trying to make an appointment with my usual hairstylist, so I just walked in.

After getting my hair shampooed, my hairstylist, Beth,

started a conversation with me as soon as I was seated in the swivel chair.

I remember her saying, "I don't know why, but I feel that I could tell you anything about myself, and I don't even know you."

As the conversation progressed, she would often pause and ask me what I thought about the events in her life.

I suppose my responses to her questions prompted her to ask me if I was psychic because she commented to me several times, "How could you know that? I didn't say anything about that."

Once the cat was out of the bag, I confessed that I had given readings professionally at one time in my life and that I really didn't do that anymore.

She said, "Oh my God! You have a gift; you shouldn't stop helping people."

I told her that I helped many people anyway because I worked as a critical care nurse.

She said, "Oh no, any regular person can do that, but not everyone can do what you just did. Don't stop using your gift."

She then told me that she had a good friend who had died six months earlier and asked me if talking to people who had died was part of my gift. I told her it was, and she asked me if I could contact her best friend. I told her I would try, but I couldn't guarantee he would come through.

Within a matter of seconds, I started seeing a young man who I perceived to be about twenty-one years old. He had black hair, brown eyes, and an olive complexion.

I described what I was seeing to Beth, and she said, "Oh my God! That's him. His name was Freddy, and he was such a sweet guy."

I asked her not to give me any more details until after my communication with him. Freddy showed me that he was shot by a man with a handgun. He said that he was at the wrong place at the wrong time and mistaken for somebody else. He told me to tell Beth not to worry about him because he was in a good place and would come back one day and do it right.

As I relayed Freddy's message to Beth, tears streamed down her face, and she said, "I never really thought he would be in a bad place because he was such a sweet soul."

She finished my haircut, and I followed her to the cash register to pay my bill. I had made it halfway to my car when she came running after me in the parking lot. "Ms. Shirley, since you were able to contact Freddy, I have to ask you if you can sense anything about my father."

Once again, I told her that I didn't know but would try. Within a matter of seconds, I started to pick up on emotions that weren't mine. Then I saw a middle-aged man sitting on a couch with a bottle of alcohol and pill bottles on a coffee table within his reach. I watched as he held his face in his hands and sobbed inconsolably. I asked him why he was so sad. He then showed me a scene from his childhood where he was dropped off at some type of military boarding school. He told me his parents left him without so much as a hug. He said he felt so alone and abandoned, and that whenever he had the school secretary call his home, no one would ever be there to answer. He showed me another scene where everyone had to march until they were all in sync, which took all day. He made me feel his exhaustion and despair and commented that the school was too demanding on little boys. The little boy I was witnessing was of grammar school age, probably around the age of eight or nine years old. He said that every night he would collapse into his bed, which was located in a large room shared by many other boys his age, and he would sob into his pillow until he fell asleep.

I looked up at Beth; she had tears streaming down her face again. She said, "You just described my dad. He had severe emotional problems and depression from the time he was a little boy, when his parents put him in a military boarding school. He committed suicide after he and my mom divorced. He overdosed on pills and alcohol."

I thought, Well, *that explains the pills and alcohol I saw in my vision.* I told her that her dad said he was in a good place now and she didn't have to worry about him. She hugged my neck, and we said our goodbyes.

I didn't think much about the reading afterwards until I received a Facebook message from Beth's mom, Liz, a few days later, requesting that I give her a reading. Beth had looked me up and made a request to be Facebook friends with me. I agreed, and I guess one thing just leads to another. Anyway, I responded in Messenger and explained that I was in the process of moving to Florida and didn't really give readings anymore. She wrote back and stated she understood and asked if I would make an exception for her because no one had ever been able to bring through her ex-husband before. I was the only one and her last hope. I wrote back to her and told her I would try to make some time after I got settled in after the move.

Well, several months went by, and I still had not contacted Beth's mom to give her the reading. My husband, Joe, and I were sitting at a nice Italian Restaurant in Sarasota when Beth's ex-husband got really pushy with me.

He said, "If you don't call my wife tonight and give her my message, I will see to it that you have no peace. I will pester you night and day. I will enter your dreams and watch everything you do!"

Needless to say, that did the trick. I told my husband while we were still eating dinner that the deceased ex-husband of a woman who had asked me for a reading was going to haunt me until I gave her his message. As soon as we left the restaurant, I wasted no time calling her. To my surprise, she answered on the first ring and began to cry.

She said, "I was hoping that you would call soon. I didn't want to bother you, but I am desperate to have some closure."

Her husband didn't waste any time communicating information to me. I saw him abusing her physically and heard him abusing her verbally as well. I told her what I was seeing and hearing as I received it. I told her I saw him pulling on her arm, and she said that he had actually broken her right forearm. I told her I heard him calling her a "stupid bitch" and using other profanities. She said he was constantly calling her names and putting her down. I told her that he had told me to tell her he was sorry for the way he treated her because he really did love her and still does. I also told her he said he takes full responsibility for his own death and that it wasn't her fault. He was emotionally ill and taking pills, and drinking alcohol didn't help the situation—it made things much worse. He said he was very sorry he had caused her so much emotional pain and anguish over his death.

At this point, Liz started to sob.

She said, "I have been living with guilt for over ten years. He wrote in his suicide note that it was my fault he was dead. He said, If I had stayed with him instead of leaving, he wouldn't have needed to kill himself."

I interjected by saying, "Liz, if you had stayed, he would have probably killed you too!"

I continued with the message by telling her he told me he was at peace and in heaven, that he asked God for forgiveness and mercy as he was dying, and God granted him entry into heaven. Liz said she was glad to hear he was at peace and in heaven. She said she had prayed many times that God would rescue him and keep him from hell. The day after the reading, Liz sent me a testimonial by way of text message to show her gratitude for the reading.

At The Nail Spa

I can't escape Spirit, even when I'm having my nails done. I was sitting at the manicurist table trying to pick out a new color for my nails when a very petite, slender, and mature Asian lady with short salt and pepper-colored hair popped into my head. She was standing in front of what looked like bamboo shoots with her arms crossed and her head tilted slightly to one side. I almost felt intimidated by her appearance; however, I asked her who she was and what she wanted.

She said, "I am the mother."

I said, "Okay, what do you want?"

She replied, "I want you to tell my daughter I am no longer angry about her leaving. Let her know that I am very proud of her. Tell her I am with her all the time, and I like the way she tried to help her siblings back home all these years. I knew she wanted to come back home to visit but didn't have the money. It's okay. I am not angry anymore. I am happy for her."

I took a deep breath and told my manicurist I was a psychic medium and I had a lady with me in Spirit who was about 4'9" tall, very tiny, with short, salt and pepper hair, and brown eyes. She had her arms crossed and was standing outside in front of what looked like bamboo shoots. I was uncertain as to why her mother had her arms crossed, so I asked her if her mother normally stood with her arms crossed.

She said, "Yes, my mother always crossed her arms."

I told her practically verbatim what her mother had told me. She continued to file my nails without expressing any emotion except for some tearing in her eyes. She asked me if her mother had anything else to say, and I told her that she didn't.

~ Eight ~

ON VACATION WITH THE SPIRITS OF ITALY

*The graves stood tenantless, and the sheeted dead
did squeak and gibber in the Roman streets.*
—William Shakespeare, *Hamlet*

The Massacre At Stresa, Italy

During our trip to Italy, we visited many wonderful and haunting places, such as the Roman Colosseum, The Circus Maximus, the Vatican, Capri, Ana Capri, Florence, Murano, Venice, Verona, Sorrento, Pisa, Pompeii, and the list goes on. For the sake of time and space, I will talk about only four locations that stood out as significant. Out of all the places we visited, Stresa was the most important for me because the spirits I encountered there followed me home.

Nestled on the shore of beautiful Lake Maggiore, Stresa

is a picturesque town in Northern Italy, south of Switzerland. As soon as our tour bus entered the city limits, I had visions of Nazi Soldiers dressed in WWII uniforms walking around and standing in the streets. I whispered to my husband that I didn't like Stresa because it felt very oppressive. I wasn't quite sure what to make of it, and I didn't ask Spirit. I didn't have any prior knowledge of exactly what happened in Italy during WWII. I initially thought maybe German Soldiers had vacationed in Stresa. I did not know they had actually occupied Italy after the fall of Mussolini.

We stayed at the beautiful and luxurious Regina Palace Hotel. This hotel had much positive residual energy left by the many VIPs who had stayed at the hotel while vacationing at Lake Maggiore, especially during the early years of the twentieth century. I didn't perceive any evil or negative acts being carried out in this hotel at all. I did have some visions of a few German officers staying at the hotel, but they didn't appear to be trying to control the guests or hotel operations. Our room was beautiful and spacious, with a luxurious bathroom. As soon as we got settled into our room, we took our showers and dressed for dinner. During our walk to the dining room, I was totally awestruck by the luxurious architecture of this grand hotel. That evening, we dined on a five-course meal and the best red wine that the Tuscan region of Italy has to offer. After much wine and socializing, we made our way back to our room. It didn't take long for me to fall asleep that evening, as I was totally exhausted.

I had distressing dreams that night, but the most

distressing dream of all occurred just before the alarm clock went off. I dreamed that a woman named Lotte was taken away with a group of about fifteen other people by Nazi soldiers to a location that seemed to be near the outskirts of a small town on Lake Maggiore. My dream revealed to me that this group of people had stayed together at the same hotel while they were on vacation, but it wasn't the Regina Palace. It was a nice hotel, but much smaller than the Regina. I don't know for sure if they were taken from Stresa or some other small town near the lake. They were transported in a canvas-covered, military-type truck to the outskirts of town and made to get off in single file. Then they were corralled into a very confined space and forced to kneel. As Lotte got down and covered her head with her hands, I realized I was witnessing this event through the eyes of a middle-aged Jewish woman who had been taken away from her husband while they were on vacation. I saw the backside of this lady as she kneeled on the ground. She had dark hair and was wearing a dark-colored dress with beige stockings that had a seam down the back of her legs. I could feel this lady's shock, disbelief, and depression related to being taken captive and separated from her husband. She knew she would probably never see him again. In all of her despair, she seemed to be more concerned about the young teenage girl crouched down on the ground beside her than she was about herself. Although these individuals were filled with fear and uncertainty, they remained very calm.

I watched as the Nazi soldier with the machine gun opened fire on the small group. As Lotte was being sprayed with bullets, I could sense what she was feeling. My legs felt as if they were being pelleted with coarse, hot sand. I experienced an intense burning sensation on my backside, starting from the calves of my legs, spreading to my back, and then my head. I perceived that Lotte initially believed the machine gun was shooting bullets, but because she did not experience any changes in consciousness, she then thought that she was only being "pelleted" with sand. She told me the Nazis used intimidation and fear tactics to control the people in the village. She said the Nazi soldier with the gun pelleted them with what felt like sand. I think she believed that maybe the group was just being intimidated. I don't believe Lotte realized she had actually been killed by a Nazi with a machine gun. Although I wasn't looking forward to the alarm going off at 5:30 in the morning when I went to bed the night before, I was happy to have it wake me from my nightmare.

This dream stayed with me the whole day, even as we traveled further north in Italy to Lake Lugano (a glacial lake situated on the border between southern Switzerland and Northern Italy) for a day trip before returning to the Regina Palace Hotel later that afternoon. On the way to Lake Lugano, I tried my best to focus on the beautiful countryside, but my mind kept wandering back to the dream. The more I obsessed about the dream, the more I realized that the middle-aged lady of my dream had become attached to me, so I decided to start a conversation with her. I asked her if she knew she was dead. She replied:

"I'm not dead. The teenage girl and I escaped the Nazis."

Her reply to me confirmed my impression—*she didn't realize she was dead.*

Then she stated, "I'm looking for my husband and can't find him anywhere."

I asked her about the young teenage girl who was with her in the dream.

Lotte said, "She is with me, and I am very concerned about her because she is always so sad."

I asked her if there was anybody else with her besides the teenage girl.

She said, "I haven't seen any of the other people in my group; I think they may have also escaped."

I told her I believed she had died with the rest of her group the day the Nazis took them away.

She replied, "I don't feel dead, so I can't be."

I told her that if she listened to me and did exactly what I said, I could possibly help reunite her with her husband.

Lotte asked, "How is that possible when I keep going

back to the hotel and my home and can never find him there, only strangers?"

I told her he wasn't in any of those places because he had already died and crossed over.

With a scowl on her face, she asked, "What do you mean by crossing over?"

I explained to her that when a soul crosses over, it returns to the Great Spirit. I told her it was like the Garden of Eden, a beautiful place filled with love and joy, and she would find her husband there.

"Well, if that's the case, tell me how I can cross over."

I told her I would create a doorway filled with the Light of Spirit that she and the teenage girl could enter into and be reunited with their friends and loved ones.

Then she said, "I think you are trying to trick me because there is no such place."

I tried to reassure her that there was such a place, and I promised her that if she believed I could get her there, then she would be able to see for herself that such a place exists.

Angrily, she said, "No way, Lady! I am not going anywhere."

> I emphatically told her that she could not stay with me. I asked her why she came to me if she didn't want my help.
>
> She meekly replied, "I could see you and felt you might become a good friend to me."
>
> I asked her if she was afraid to cross over.
>
> She said, "I was taught that dead people go to Sheol, and I don't want to go there."
>
> I told her the Garden of Eden existed and she could go there to find her husband.
>
> Once again, she told me, "I'm not going to leave."
>
> I told her that her place was no longer on earth.
>
> She sarcastically replied, "My place is wherever I want it to be!"

I knew then that I had my work cut out for me. This spirit had become attached to me and was not going to let go easily. I knew that as soon as I got back home to Florida, I would have to call on some of my spiritual Jewish friends and have them help me cross Lotte and her teenage charge over into a good place.

By the time we flew back to the States, Lotte had completely attached herself to me, making me feel her despair and causing me to become despondent and distant from my own husband. I was withdrawn and irritable. Lotte's spirit completely overwhelmed me. As if it wasn't bad enough that I had Lotte attached to me, the teenager also started to channel her emotions through me. The teenager made me feel her intense sadness and grief because she would never grow up and marry the man of her dreams. She was going to miss all the romantic moments of dating and being married. She felt cheated, sad, and angry all at the same time. I found myself crying frequently. This teenage girl attached herself to me along with Lotte. I have never had one spirit, much less two, attach to me before. I knew I needed help soon.

My dream occurred on the morning of October 2, 2019. We flew home from Milan, Italy, on the afternoon of October 3. We finally arrived home at about one o'clock on the morning of October 4th. The spirits of Lotte and the teenage girl stayed with me from the morning of my dream until the evening of my Psychic Practice Circle on October 8th, which, ironically, was the date of Yom Kippur for 2019.

Every Tuesday evening, I lead a psychic development group and was planning on getting some of my Jewish participants to help me cross Lotte and the teenage girl over that evening. I called Devin that afternoon to let her know what I was planning. I explained to her what had happened towards the end of my vacation, and I told her I needed her help in crossing over the two Jewish souls attached to me because I had been unsuccessful at crossing them over myself. She said she would love to help me; however, it was Yom Kippur, and she wouldn't be able to attend the circle that evening. I asked her what Yom Kippur was. She said it was the day that Jewish people fasted and said prayers for the atonement of their sins, so they could seal their fate for the upcoming year. While Devin was explaining Yom Kippur to me, she paused, gasped, and said that they also recited prayers for the dead so that they could gain entry into Gan Eden (the Garden of Eden or Paradise). Devin commented about how creepy it was for these two souls to attach themselves to me and follow me back to the U.S. just days before Yom Kippur. She said it was as if they knew I would be able to get help for them. She said she would say the Yizkor for them that evening, which is a prayer recited for forgiveness for the dead.

After my conversation with Devin, I did some research online and discovered the prayers and rituals associated with Yom Kippur. I downloaded and printed a copy of the prayer for the dead, and then I went shopping to see if I could find a Yahrzeit candle. I couldn't find the Yahrzeit candle, so I bought a white luminara candle as a substitute (which, as I discovered from my research, was an acceptable alternative). I was disappointed that Devin wouldn't be able to attend the circle that evening, but I was hoping one of my other Jewish participants would. If not, I would have to light a candle, recite the prayers, and try to cross Lotte and the teenager over with the help of my psychic circle buddies. Fortunately, at the psychic circle that evening, I had one Jewish participant, Margaret, who decided to come to the circle instead of attending the synagogue. She momentarily lamented her choice to come to the circle instead of the synagogue before I interrupted and told her that it was meant for her to be there with us that evening so that she could recite the Yizkor to help cross over the two Jewish souls that had attached to me. I told her it was possible that the group could cross them over, but we would more likely be successful if we gained the trust and cooperation needed from Lotte and the teenager by having one of their own kindred souls light the candle and say the prayers. Margaret played the Hebrew translation of the Yizkor on her cell phone, and we all visualized an open portal of light with Lotte and the teenager stepping through into Paradise. After the prayers and visualization, we all felt a shift in the room, and my group noticed a change in my countenance. They all said I didn't look like the same person who had come into the room earlier that evening. They said I looked like myself again, and my countenance had changed from dark and depressing to light and joyful. I definitely felt the shift in my mood and immediately knew that Lotte and the teenager had crossed over into Gan Eden.

The Yizkor may be said for all Jewish dead: parents, grandparents, mates, children, family, and friends. It may be recited for suicides and for sinners. The living can redeem the dead. Atonement must be sought for both. Technically, the name for the *Day of Atonement* should be written in the plural, *atonements,* because on that day the Jew must seek atonement for both those who are present and those who sleep in the dust. The following prayer is the English translation of the prayer that Margaret played:

Merciful God in Heaven, grant perfect repose to the soul of _____ who has passed to her eternal habitation; and in whose memory, the members of her family pledge charity. May she be under Thy divine wings among the holy and pure who shine bright as the sky; may her place of rest be in paradise. Merciful One, keep her soul forever alive under Thy protective wings. The Lord being her heritage, may she rest in peace; and let us say, Amen.

Prayer alone may not be sufficient for a dignified and meaningful memorial. It must be accompanied by an act of charity, a personal, material demonstration of kindness. The Yizkor came to be recited on major holidays when Deuteronomy 15–16 is read, which contains the phrase, "Each man shall give according to his ability." Those chapters command man to be charitable, to support the poor, the orphan, the widow, and the Levites who depend on his graciousness. The proper memorial service contains a phrase denoting a sum of charity that is being pledged. This statement should not be taken lightly; it is not a mere liturgical formula. If no charity will be given, it should not be included. It is preferable not to promise at all than to renege on a vow. Thus, the Yizkor prayer recited on Yom Kippur includes both prayer and an act of charity.

On October 11th, I did a fundraiser event for charity at WKDW, 97.5 FM, in North Port, Florida. At the time, WKDW broadcasted my weekly radio show called *Spirit Speak*s. At this fundraising event, I gave messages from Spirit to a group of about seventy people. This event had been planned several months earlier. I am not Jewish, and

I had definitely not intended to perform any type of charitable act such as a fundraiser as a part of the rites related to Yom Kippur, but, ironically, it worked out that way. I can't help but feel that Providence somehow worked out everything as it should be so that the redemption of Lotte and the young teenage girl would be sealed for eternity. I feel Lotte has been reunited with her husband in the Garden of Eden, and the teenage girl is experiencing romance with a handsome young man who was also taken too soon. God does work in mysterious ways!

Spirits At The Catacombs Of Domitilla

The Catacombs of Domitilla, located in Rome, Italy, are a network of underground early Christian and pagan cemeteries named after the Domitilla family, which is responsible for having them dug. The catacombs were created out of tufa stone, a soft stone of volcanic origin on which the whole of Rome is built. Sometimes the burial galleries were obtained by reusing already existing passageways (water conduits or quarries) or, as happened most often, they were freshly dug out of the tufa. The oldest tombs exist higher up in the catacombs. When space started to run out, the gravediggers lowered the floor level by creating different stories, one above the other, with connecting stairways. The Catacombs of Santa Domitilla are the oldest and most extensive network of catacombs. Only five of the sixty catacombs are open to the public. They are located 16 meters underground, span an area of 15 kilometers (7.4 miles), have four levels of labyrinths, and have a total of 26,250 tombs. These catacombs were actively used as a cemetery from around the first through fifth centuries CE and were rediscovered in 1593 by the archaeologist Antonio Bosio. The renovated areas include frescoes from both pagan mythology and the Christian faith, showing how intertwined the two were in the early Church. The first area restored without the use of lasers dates back to the third century and still displays many frescoes of pagan art, from grape vines adorning the vaults of the passages to the cupids used for the smaller tombs, most likely belonging to children. During the Middle Ages, many of the crypts had frescoes that appeared to have been blotted out but were actually stripped by "ripping" when the catacombs were looted and the frescoes were cut out and removed as trophies. This ancient form of art theft can be found in a museum in Catania, which displays examples originally brought to Sicily by a nobleman to decorate his home.

We were fortunate to have an excellent tour guide for the Catacombs of Domitilla. She grew up in Rome and earned a degree in history from one of the local universities. Not only did she have in-depth knowledge of the Catacombs, but she was very passionate about their history. Initially, I was a little apprehensive about touring the underground graves. I didn't know exactly what I might encounter down there. I took some comfort in knowing that the area of the catacombs we would be touring was the burial place of Martyrs and early Christians who I perceived to be good souls. After listening to a lecture given in the Basilica of San Clemente about the history of early

Christianity and the Martyrs buried in the Catacombs, we began the tour.

As we descended the steps to the city of the dead, I felt I had been sucked up into the eye of a spiritual tornado, a place of calm but with powerful, intense energy swirling around me. Although no remains were left in the catacombs we explored, I could feel the presence of souls sleeping nearby. The faith these souls have in the power of Christ to resurrect their physical bodies is so strong that it permeates the ether. I have never perceived such strong faith before in my entire life. I felt this was such a holy and sacred place that even the most ancient of evil forces could not prevail. Believe me when I tell you that the faith of these early Christians and martyrs triumphed over the most ancient evil energies imaginable. I could feel its presence as a force that was still present but totally restrained because of the strong faith of these souls. This evil force may have robbed these Christian martyrs of their physical lives, but it could not rob them of their souls. I felt a sense of relief as we ascended the stairs and re-entered the basilica. The energy in the catacombs felt thick and overwhelming as compared to the energy in the basilica, which felt light and airy.

Pompeii Is Full Of The Spirits Of The Dead

Pompeii is an ancient Roman city located along the shore of the Bay of Naples in the Campania region of Italy. Pompeii, along with Herculaneum and many other towns in the surrounding area, was buried under 4 to 6 meters of volcanic ash and pumice in the eruption of Mount Vesuvius in 79 AD. Of the 20,000 inhabitants in the city at the time, the estimate is that all but about 2,000 unfortunate souls escaped unharmed, while Pompeii was left buried by over 19 feet of volcanic ash and pumice. When excavations began in 1748, entire villas complete with intricate mosaics and frescoes emerged almost intact. Plaster casts of those poor souls who died could be seen frozen in time. The most minute details of an individual's life were laid bare.

On the morning of August 24, 79 AD, Mount Vesuvius began spewing fire and smoke. Originally, it may have seemed that the mountain was doing nothing more than offering a harmless pyrotechnic display; however, by midday, Mount Vesuvius erupted with an explosion that blew off the entire top of the mountain. A massive mushroom cloud of pumice particles rose approximately 27 miles (43 km) into the sky. The power of the explosion has been calculated as being 100,000 times greater than the nuclear bomb that devastated Hiroshima in 1945. The ash that first rained down on Pompeii was light in weight, but the density was such that within a few minutes everything was covered in inches of it. There is evidence that people tried to flee the town or sought shelter where they could, and those without shelter tried in vain to keep themselves above the shifting layers of volcanic material. By late afternoon, a second massive explosion filled the air, sending a pillar of ash even higher than the previous cloud. This ash was much heavier than the first eruption, and the volcanic material that smothered the town was several feet thicker than before. While victims huddled near walls and under stairs in an attempt to seek protection—some hugging their loved ones or clasping their most precious possessions—buildings collapsed under the accumulated weight of the ash. Later that night, the huge cloud hanging above the volcano collapsed from its own weight and blasted the town in six devastating waves of superheated ash and air, which asphyxiated and literally baked the bodies of the entire population that was left behind. The ash continued falling, and the once vibrant city was buried.

In the usual Roman fashion, the town was surrounded by a wall with many gates, often with two or three arched entrances to separate pedestrians from vehicle traffic. Within the walls, there were wide, paved streets, but there were no street names or numbers. The city contained an astonishing mix of several thousand buildings, including small and large homes, villas, shops, temples, baths, schools, taverns, a pottery shop, an exercise ground, an arena, public toilettes, water towers, about forty fountains, a market hall, a plant and flower nursery, fulleries, a basilica, brothels, and theaters. Also included were hundreds of small shrines to all kinds of deities and ancestors. In short, Pompeii had all the amenities you would expect to find in a thriving community. Preserved by the eruption, this once prosperous commercial port town offers a unique glimpse into the everyday life of the ancient Romans.

Pompeii had many large villas, most of which were built in the 2nd century BCE, that display the Greek colonial origins of the town. The typical entrance of these plush residences was a small street doorway with an entrance corridor that opened into a large columned atrium with a rectangular pool of water open to the sky and from which other rooms, for example, a bedroom or dining room, were accessed. Movable screens, often decorated with mythological scenes, were used to separate rooms. During the winter, these screens were also used to help keep in the heat provided by braziers. Another common feature was a hall space where valuables were kept. There was also a place reserved in the home for ancestor worship, which was a large part of Roman family life. A striking feature of these Pompeian homes was the magnificent floor mosaics depicting all kinds of scenes. For example, a mosaic was discovered in a home owned by a businessman that proudly proclaims that "Profit is Joy." Many houses had a private garden with statues, ornate fountains, vine-covered pergolas, and canvas awnings, all surrounded by a peristyle. Many private residences also had areas dedicated to viniculture, the production of grapes for making wine.

The House of Faun is a good example of the typical grander residence of Pompeii. Most of the larger villas also had an eating area in the garden so that guests could dine outside on cushioned benches. Some of these villas also had a system of small canals running between the diners so that as dishes floated past, they could take their pick of the delicacies that were being served. Villas without gardens often use wall paintings to give the illusion of landscape vistas. The wall paintings from these residences have given great insight into areas of Pompeian life such as sex, diet, clothes, religion, architecture, industry, and agriculture. They also revealed the status of guests because the seating was formally arranged so that the most important guest ascended as one went clockwise around the circle of diners. Sometimes the wall painting reflected the status of the guest who ate in front of it. More modest structures included basic two- or sometimes three-story residences, simple taverns, and brothels, which contained nothing more than curtained cubicles. In complete contrast to the richer residences, slave quarters have also survived, and they show the cramped, prison-like existence of this large section of the population.

What can I say about Pompeii other than that I was totally mesmerized? I encountered many spirits while walking the cobblestone streets. Every square centimeter of the ancient city seemed to be occupied by the souls of those who lived and died there long ago. Many of these souls died during the eruption of Mt. Vesuvius, but most had died long before. I was in awe of the complexities of this ancient city. I perceived an overwhelming mix of feelings as I walked the well-trodden ancient streets. In some sections of the town, I felt happy and free; in other sections, I felt sad and enslaved; and as I continued to walk, I experienced areas where I felt pleasant, angry, and even horrified. The views of the frescoes and mosaics contained in most of the grander homes were breathtaking. I perceived a class-oriented society in which middle- and upper-class citizens experienced Utopia, while lower-class and enslaved individuals experienced a life of hardship.

The sexual energy there permeated the air. I perceived

that sex was definitely a very important part of the daily lives of the Pompeians. As we toured some of the baths, I was given visions of people in different heterosexual and homosexual acts. Most of these people were fully grown, men and women. However, there were many young boys and girls around the age of ten to twelve who were involved in sexual acts with each other or older individuals. I was repulsed by many of these acts, especially the ones involving children. I was told that they weren't too young for sex because they were of marrying age. Also, many of these children were sex slaves and had no choice in the matter. Most of them were born into slavery and came to embrace their position as sex slaves because they received better overall treatment than their child counterparts, who endured hard labor every day of their short lives. Unfortunately, even in modern times, sexual abuse of children occurs all over the globe, and (at the time of this writing) all types of human trafficking of children are on the rise. According to the National Center for Missing & Exploited Children (NCMEC), child sex trafficking is a form of child abuse that occurs when a child under 18 is advertised, solicited, or exploited through a commercial sex act. A commercial sex act is any sex act where something of value—such as money, food, drugs, or a place to stay—is given to or received by any person for sexual activity. If you suspect that a child may be the victim of human trafficking or sexual abuse, please contact your local authorities, make a report to NCMEC's CyberTipline, or call 1-800-THE-LOST.

I was totally disturbed by the brutal treatment of

some of their slaves, especially those assigned to do hard labor. I had many visions of their cramped housing and squalid living conditions. These slaves were comprised of both fair-skinned and olive-complected individuals. Some looked as if they could have been German, some looked Greek, and others looked Spanish or Roman. I was told that these people became slaves because of debts they or their families owed or because they were criminals or captives of war.

During my walk, I perceived that the Pompeians were pious in their religious beliefs and showed their gratitude for prosperity and protection through a variety of sacrifices such as cakes, wine, fruit, and the occasional animal. I was relieved that I didn't perceive any human sacrifice. Temples and altars offer evidence of their religious beliefs and practices. Because Pompeii was a port of trade, ships, and foreign vessels brought new religions to the land. Archaeological evidence suggests that the Pompeians preferred the goddess Venus, protector of Pompeii. The gods Lares and Penates—protectors of households—were also worshiped by homeowners in Pompeii and Herculaneum.

As we walked down the path leading away from the excavation site, I was made to feel how the Pompeians suffered as they lay dying after the eruption. The last moments of life in Pompeii were horrific. I felt as if I was smothering and burning all at the same time. I also felt betrayed by the Goddess Venus; maybe my bountiful sacrifices had not been adequate and I was somehow being punished for my lack of gratitude. After the tour, we had lunch at a restaurant across the street from the excavation site. I was extremely relieved when we finally loaded the bus after dinner and returned to Sorrento. I was in total awe of Pompeii but totally overwhelmed by the great number of spirits remaining there.

Spilled Blood Speaks Of The Horrors At The Rome Colosseum

The Roman Colosseum, also known as the Flavian Amphitheater, was the largest amphitheater in the Roman world, measuring some 620 by 513 feet, or 190 by 155 meters. The Colosseum was a freestanding structure made of stone and concrete. Most other amphitheaters of the period were dug into a hillside to provide adequate support. The exterior had three stories of arched entryways—a total of eighty—that were supported by semi-circular columns. Near the main entrance to the Colosseum stands the Arch of Constantine, built in A.D. 315 to honor Constantine I's victory over Maxentius at Pons Milvius.

The Colosseum had seating for about 50,000 spectators, arranged according to social ranking. Awnings were unfurled from the top story to protect the audience from the heat of the sun as they watched the spectacle below. These shows often lasted from dawn until nightfall, and the gladiators usually kicked off the show with a chariot procession accompanied by trumpets and a hydraulic organ. Fantasy duels often began the day's combat events; these were usually fought between dwarfs, women, or the disabled using wooden weapons. Blood sports between various classes of gladiators, including females, were fought with weapons such as swords, lances, tridents, and nets. Gladiators were generally slaves, condemned criminals, or prisoners of war.

Next came the animal hunts with the bestiarii—the professional beast killers. The animals had no chance in these contests. They were most often killed at a distance using spears or arrows. Dangerous animals such as lions, tigers, bears, elephants, leopards, hippopotamuses, and bulls were placed in the arena with defenseless animals such as deer, ostriches, and giraffes. These defenseless animals did not stand a chance against the dangerous animals. Hundreds, sometimes even thousands, of animals were butchered in a single day's event, often brutally. The brutality was deliberate to achieve *crudeness*—the correct amount of cruelty.

Under Domitian, dramas were also held in the Colosseum, but with a bloodthirsty realism, such as using condemned prisoners for executions; a real Hercules was burned on a funeral pyre; and a prisoner was actually crucified. The Colosseum was also the scene of many executions during the lunchtime lull, particularly the killing of Christian martyrs. Much debate, however, exists as to whether or not Christians were actually martyred in the Colosseum or outside the city. Regardless of where they were martyred, Christians were seen as an unacceptable challenge to the authority of Pagan Rome and the divinity of the Emperor. They were thrown to the lions, shot down with arrows, roasted alive, or killed in a myriad of cruelly inventive ways.

The Colosseum saw over four centuries of active use until the struggles of the Western Roman Empire and the gradual change in public tastes put an end to gladiatorial combats by the 6th century A.D. Even by that time, the arena had suffered damage due to lightning strikes and earthquakes. In the centuries to come, the Colosseum was abandoned completely and used as a quarry for different building projects, including the cathedrals of St. Peter and St. John Lateran, the Palazzo Venezia, and defense fortifications along the Tiber River. Beginning in the 18th century, various popes sought to conserve the arena as a sacred Christian site, though it is in fact uncertain whether early Christian martyrs actually met their fate in the Colosseum, as has been speculated. By the 20th century, a combination of neglect, vandalism, weather, and natural disasters had destroyed nearly two-thirds of the original Colosseum, including all of the arena's marble seats and its decorative elements. Efforts to restore the Colosseum began in the 1990s and have progressed over the years. The Colosseum is a leading attraction for tourists from all over the world.

From the moment my husband and I entered the Colosseum grounds, I started receiving impressions. I saw Roman citizens clad in ancient garb walking around and congregating in small groups. I also saw statues that were no longer there. While standing in line to enter the Colosseum, I saw horses pulling open wagons full of metal scraps away from the amphitheater. In another scene, I also saw horses pulling closed wagons with bars filled with either people or animals into the amphitheater. We had the opportunity to go into the basement, but I refused. There was no way I could stand the dark energy I perceived down there. We toured the first level of the Colosseum, which was more than enough for me. From the first level, we were able to see the rooms that existed below what was once the platform or floor of the arena. This is where they kept the gladiators, criminals, and animals waiting to be put on display that day. From what I understand, the floor stayed saturated with the massive amount of blood shed every day. I believe it because the stains can still be seen on the stones that supported the wooden floor of the arena. As I gazed down into the maze of rooms below, I could see rooms that held passive animals, dangerous animals, male gladiators, female gladiators, male prisoners, and female prisoners.

When I returned my gaze to the top of the blood-stained stones, towards my right field of vision, I received a psychic vision of a young woman with disheveled long black hair who was backed up against a stone wall. She was wearing scanty, dirty-looking rags that barely covered her breasts and genitalia. There was a look of terror on her face that I don't think I'll ever forget. I could feel her sense of helplessness as well as her desire for a quick death. I looked to my left to see what was causing her so much horror. Several lions had just been released from a cage in the stone wall and were walking slowly towards her. I watched as the lions surrounded her and knocked her to the ground. I heard her scream once when they first attacked her, and then it was over. One by one, each lion ripped the flesh from various parts of her body, ultimately tearing her apart limb by limb. I feel that her soul left her body long before she died from the attack, or at least I hope so. I don't believe her spirit is haunting the Colosseum. I think what I saw was residual energy playing in my head like a movie. The land and physical structures hold a lot of this energy, and the blood-stained stones are saturated with it. I can't say for sure if this young lady was a Christian martyr or not because I wasn't told, but I was made to feel that she had not committed a crime. She was an innocent victim.

I had several other visions while we were touring the Colosseum that were equally disturbing. I saw animals fighting each other to the death, men killing animals with spears and swords, and men being crucified or executed in some other cruel manner. There were seesaws that flung men about fifteen feet in the air. These men landed so hard on the platform that their heads were crushed and their limbs were twisted and broken. After about an hour of touring, I couldn't take it anymore. I told my husband I had to get out of there. We didn't explore any further than the entry-level of the amphitheater. I am glad I was able to visit this ancient site with my husband, but it is definitely not on my list of things to do again. The visions I experienced there were extremely overwhelming.

~ Nine ~

SPIRITS OF RELATIVES WHO SAID GOODBYE

The living owe it to those who no longer can speak to tell their story for them.
— Czesław Miłosz, *The Issa Valley*

Great Uncle Joe Can Wear Shoes Again

Great Uncle Joe was one of my Grandma Nora's older brothers and the fourth child to be born out of twelve children. He contracted gangrene in both of his legs due to uncontrolled diabetes and had to have them amputated above the knees. He suffered for many years in a nursing home before he finally passed away. Uncle Joe had been married and had several children. His wife divorced him after he lost his legs and livelihood, taking their five children with her. She and the children visited him periodically in the nursing home, even after she remarried; however, these visits were few and far between. My grandma would visit Uncle Joe often, along with her youngest sister, Sofia.

I went along on one of those visits when I was a child, and it scared me so much that I never went with her again. The image of him lying in bed with no legs and a look of quiet despair on his face was more than I could stand. And, if that wasn't bad enough, I could feel his intense sadness, which left me wanting to cry at the horror of his condition. I was about eight years old when I visited Uncle Joe in the nursing home with my grandmother. Even at that tender age, I remember being extremely sensitive to the emotions of others. Many years would pass before I would come to understand that I was an empath. Meanwhile, I was told I was far too sensitive to the feelings of others and shouldn't be feeling what others were feeling.

I was twelve years old when Uncle Joe came to visit me. Several years had passed since I last visited him in the nursing home with my grandmother. This would be the last time I would see him because this was a good-bye visit. It wasn't a visit in the normal sense—it was a ghostly visit. I was sitting in my favorite overstuffed chair reading one of Alfred Hitchcock's thrillers when Uncle Joe appeared to me in a vision from out of nowhere. I certainly wasn't thinking about him, as I was totally fixated on my book. Great Uncle Joe showed himself to me as a whole and healthy person. He was sitting on the side of his hospital bed with both feet and legs intact, as if they had never been amputated.

He bent over to put his shoes on, and as he was tying

his shoelaces, he looked up at me as if I were standing directly in front of him and said, "Tell Nora that I have to be going soon, but we'll see each other again someday. Let her know that I can wear my shoes again."

After he made these statements, he smiled as he stood up, turned to his left, walked through an archway, and up a flight of stairs. The stairway was filled with a bluish-white pearlescent light that seemed to beckon Uncle Joe to enter. I watched as he ascended the stairs, never looking back.

I went to the kitchen, where I found my grandma with her friend Rose. I told her about the vision and gave her the message from Uncle Joe. I was immediately reprimanded by Rose, whose comments were very hurtful. The most hurtful one was, "You stop that; that comes from the devil, and you are a witch. That's Satanism." My reply to her was, "I am neither a witch nor a Satanist. I love God, and I go to Sunday School every week."

That incident had a profound impact on me, which stayed with me for a long time. At that moment, I realized I would have to be careful about what I said in front of people outside my own family. Within three days, my grandma received the news that Uncle Joe had died. This was the first of many prophetic messages about upcoming transitions from my maternal grandmother's siblings. All of my grandma's siblings who died before she did paid me a visit either before or immediately after their transition into the afterlife.

Don't Worry About Gina!

My great-aunt Maria was the second child born out of the twelve children who had been born and survived. She was the oldest girl, ten years older than my grandmother. Aunt Maria had five children, and all of them were perfectly healthy, with the exception of her firstborn. Gina was born with hydrocephalus, a condition characterized by an abnormal increase in the amount of fluid in the cranium, causing enlargement of the head and deterioration of the brain. In the 1920s, not much could be done for this condition. Gina was never able to walk and spent her life bed-bound. It was considered a miracle that she survived after birth, and a bigger miracle that she lived to reach her early seventies. Aunt Maria was a dedicated and loving mother. She cared for Gina in her small wood-framed house from the time she gave birth to her until the day she died. She worked tirelessly to give her daughter the best care. Gina never had decubitus ulcers because her mother repositioned her often and kept her skin healthy and in good condition.

About two weeks before Aunt Maria died, she visited me in my sleep. In a dream, she showed me an empty rocking chair with her walking cane leaning against the wall behind it. I recognized this room as Gina's bedroom and the rocking chair as belonging to Aunt Maria. She would rock in this chair every evening as she read the Bible to Gina. Behind me, I heard Aunt Maria's voice say, "Tell Nora that I have to be leaving soon, but not to worry about Gina, because she will be okay."

Growing up, I recall my grandma frequently commenting that she did not know what would become of Gina if Aunt Maria were to die. The two had been inseparable from the time Gina was born. I believe Aunt Maria and Gina had a special bond that neither one of them shared with anyone else. The next day, I went by my grandmother's house and told her about the dream. She listened but didn't say a whole lot. About two weeks later, my grandma called me and told me that Aunt Maria had died in her sleep. She went on to say that she didn't know what would happen to Gina. If none of her siblings could take care of her, she would probably be put in a nursing home. I reminded my grandma about what Aunt Maria had said—not to worry about Gina because she would be okay. Gina did go to a nursing home, where she lingered in mourning for her mother for almost a year before passing away. I believe Great Aunt Maria and Gina's main purpose in their incarnation together was to experience unconditional love.

Great Uncle David Says Hello And Goodbye

My great-uncle David was a couple of years younger than my grandma. He had a wife and family of his own but remained close to his father and mother, who lived only a couple of houses down. My grandma and Uncle David were very close growing up. Grandma always felt like the older, more protective sister, and Uncle David looked to my grandma for advice and guidance throughout their childhood years. Once they reached adulthood, got married, and had families of their own, the closeness of their relationship diminished. Over the years, they did keep in touch with one another periodically by phone. I never met Uncle David face-to-face. I did see a picture of him and my grandma when they were toddlers. They could have been identical twins. They were so cute in their 1910s attire: David in his sailor suit shirt and knickerbockers, and my grandma in her pretty little floral print dress with a ribbon around the waist and a ribbon in her hair. They both had short, black hair and brown eyes. Although I had never been officially introduced to my great-uncle David, that would change one night as he visited me in my sleep. In my dream, he was sitting in a rocking chair on the front porch of his Victorian-style home.

As he rocked back and forth, he said, "Hello, my name is David, and I am your grandma Nora's younger brother. Tell her I will be leaving soon to be with Mama and not to be sad about my leaving because we will see each other again one day."

The dream ended after his message, and my eyes immediately flew open. I called my grandma that morning and told her about the dream. Two weeks later, my grandma called and told me that David had passed away. I wanted to go with her to the funeral so that I could say hello and goodbye to Great Uncle David in person, but because of the nature of my job as a nurse, I couldn't take the day off to go. Nevertheless, I felt as if I had said hello and goodbye to him in the dream visitation. I'm sure we'll meet spirit-to-spirit one day when we are all gathered by the eternal river of life.

Shall We Gather By The River?

Although my great-aunt Mertie was two years older than my grandma, she was definitely younger in spirit. Despite having experienced her share of heartache and disappointment in life, Aunt Mertie maintained an infectious sense of humor. She was devastated when her husband, who was the love of her life, left her for a much younger woman. Eventually, she was able to move on and find love again with a much younger man, whom she married. This husband was faithful to her until the day she died. He lovingly took care of her during her entire illness, never leaving her side. Aunt Mertie suffered from colon cancer for several years before going into remission for over a decade and then relapsing about a year before she died. The surgeon resected most of her colon during her first bout with cancer, and she received a course of chemotherapy as well. She took another round of chemotherapy during her relapse that didn't wipe out the cancer. It just made her feel weak. While we all knew that Mertie's cancer had returned, we did not realize how much the cancer had progressed because she masked her illness so well. She appeared to be somewhat stronger and in good spirits the last time I saw her, which was about three weeks before she passed away.

I was somewhat surprised to receive a ghostly visit from her. At about five o'clock in the morning, while I was getting ready to go to work, she stopped by to say goodbye. I was standing in front of the mirror in my bathroom applying eye makeup when I started hearing organ and piano church music playing while a vocalist sang the religious song, *Shall We Gather By The River?* I recognized the voice as belonging to Aunt Mertie. I dropped my mascara into the sink out of sheer shock. Aunt Mertie had played both the piano and organ in church in addition to singing solos. It wasn't hearing her voice that shocked me as much as the message contained in the lyrics of the song. Those lyrics meant only one thing: Aunt Mertie had passed away and was paying me a visit to say goodbye and to let me know that we would see each other again when we meet by the river of life. I thanked her for the visit and told her that I would greatly miss her. She told me that all I had to do was call out to her, and she would come to me. As soon as my visit with Aunt Mertie was over, I ran to the phone and called my grandma. When she answered, I told her about my visit from Aunt Mertie. My grandma said that Aunt Mertie had passed away about three o'clock that morning, and she was going to call me later in the day when she knew I was up. Needless to say, my grandma wasn't surprised by my call, as she acknowledged my gift but never encouraged it. Now that I think about it, I realize Aunt Mertie must have had psychic and mediumistic abilities too. My mind went back to the time we visited her after my vision of the man who supposedly broke into our house. I recalled her talking about the discerning of spirits to my mother, and she always seemed to migrate toward me. She never openly confessed her own abilities to me, but she seemed to favor me, treating me as if I were special.

Aunt Dora Is Clothing The Children In Heaven With Love!

No one had a bigger heart or smile than my great-aunt Dora. She was one of the most giving and loving people that I have ever known. I spent several summers with Aunt Dora, my cousin Donna Marie, and her epileptic brother, Carlo, in their two-story country home. Every spring, my Aunt Dora planted a huge vegetable garden filled with peas, beans, corn, tomatoes, cucumbers, and melons. She also kept an herb garden filled with lavender, rosemary, oregano, basil, and thyme. Of course, with the exception of the lavender, she used these herbs in her cooking. She would make cute little sachet bags and fill them with lavender. Then she would place them in all of the clothes drawers and closets. Wild blackberries covered the fence that surrounded her large backyard. I remember helping her preserve the blackberries and can tomatoes and other vegetables.

She also made her own pasta by hand. She didn't own any fancy machines. She made the dough with a mountain of flour, in which she created a crater and filled it with eggs. She kneaded it with the palms and heels of her hands, and when the dough mixture was firm, she rolled it out with what seemed like a three-foot rolling pin. She rolled the dough until she could see the outline of her hand on the other side of it. Like my grandma, she would cut the dough depending on how she wanted to use it. If she wanted stuffed noodles, she would cut the dough into squares with a long metal cutting device that had handles raised on both ends. She would then place a dollop of the stuffing mixture on each square and fold it over, crimping the edges of the pasta with her fingers. If she wanted spaghetti-like noodles, she would roll the prepared dough with her hands into a long log and cut it into very thin strips with a large knife. Then, she would gently roll the strands of pasta with her fingers against the flat surface of the table. When she was ready to cook the fresh spaghetti noodles, she would take the strips and drop them piece by piece into a boiling pot of water.

Aunt Dora made other kinds of noodles as well—fettuccine, linguine, and bow ties. If she had leftover fresh long noodles, she would bundle them up into little nests by wrapping them around her fingers. Then she placed them on a glass or ceramic platter to dry. When she had leftover lasagna noodles, she would hang them over a wooden rack to dry. Once the excess noodles had dried, she would put them in large glass jars and cover them with a tight-fitting lid. Sometimes she put lasagna noodles into a boiling pot of chicken that she had just stewed. This was my favorite pasta dish with chicken. I learned that other Southern families in the U.S. knew this dish as chicken pastry. Of course, in my mind, not all chicken pastries are equal. The pasta has to be a certain thinness to pass the litmus test for chicken pastry. Over the years, I've encountered some southern cooks who make a product with thick, biscuit-like dough. This is not chicken pasta or pastry. It is chicken dumplings, and it was influenced by German and English cooking, not Italian. Aunt Dora enjoyed cooking and made delicious meals that could easily feed an army.

Her blackberry cobbler was light and rich, definitely second to none. A couple of hours after dinner (as if dinner, including dessert, wasn't enough!) she would make huge popcorn balls with caramel and nuts, which we would feast on while we watched television. With all of this eating, you would think that we would all be very obese, but nothing could be further from the truth. We all got a lot of physical exercise just by doing our daily chores.

The only activity Aunt Dora enjoyed more than gardening, canning, and cooking was sewing. Every summer I stayed with her, I became the proud owner of tailor-made summer clothes. After she took my measurements, she would stand at her work table and draw my new shorts, top, or dress onto tissue paper using the measurements she had just taken. She would then pin the tissue paper to the fabric and cut out the pattern. When she was done sewing all the pieces together, I would have another original outfit to wear that was second to none. The clothes she made for me were so pretty, I don't think anything offered in the department stores at the time could even compare. As I grew into my early teens, I didn't visit my Aunt Dora during the summers anymore. I had a social life at home and friends with whom I wanted to go to the movies or go skating. Many years would pass before Aunt Dora would visit me in a dream. In my dream, she was sitting at her sewing machine, making clothes for children. She stopped what she was doing, looked up at me, smiled, and said, "I must be going soon. I have a job making clothes for the children in heaven."

At the time of the dream, I was not aware that Aunt

Dora had just been diagnosed with a brain tumor. That morning, I called my grandma and asked her if she had heard anything about Aunt Dora being sick. She said she had just received a phone call from Donna Marie saying Aunt Dora was in the hospital because she was having severe headaches and was passing out frequently. She went on to say they had discovered a large brain tumor that was advanced and inoperable. One week later, my Aunt Dora started her new job in heaven, making clothes for the children. I love you, Aunt Dora. Thank you for the love you clothed me with. You were truly a remarkable woman, mother, and aunt. Now, you are counted among the saints.

~ Ten ~

SPIRITS IN MY READING ROOM

The dead could only speak through the mouths of those left behind, and through the signs they left scattered behind them.
— Robert Galbraith

I Will Have Sex!

I will never forget the day I had the pleasure of doing a reading for a young elementary school principal named Tanya. She had completed her Master's Degree in Education a year earlier and had just been promoted from a third-grade teacher to principal of the same elementary school. She was single and looking for the right man with whom to spend her life, so she came to me for insight and help with her love life. I prefer to receive from Spirit what it is that my client needs in their reading, so Tanya did not tell me beforehand what type of reading she wanted. I just started giving her my impressions, as I usually do with all of my readings. I told her I perceived there was a young man in her life, and she wanted to know if he was going to propose. She squirmed and giggled with excitement, saying, "That's exactly why I'm here." The excitement of this moment was quickly brought to a halt when five of her female ancestors showed up. I told her I was seeing five women standing behind her in a semicircle. I described their physical appearances one by one, starting from my left and going to my right. The well-nourished lady to my far left introduced herself as the great-grandmother. The lady next to her introduced herself as the grandmother. The lady in the middle said she was the mother, and the two on the very end said they were her aunties. The great-grandmother told me to tell her great-granddaughter that they wanted to talk about her education and career.

Tanya pushed herself away from the table, stood up, and angrily shouted, "They show up every time I have a reading. You tell them that I don't want to talk about my education or career! I am not going to do things their way! I am done with my education! I'm going to have romance and sex—a lot of sex! Unlike them, I'm going to get married, and then I'll have babies! I'm not going to be anybody's baby mama! I'm going to do things my way! You tell them what I said!"

I told her I didn't have to tell them because they heard her.

She sat down and said, "Now, I want to talk about my love life."

We continued with her reading, and immediately I

started receiving visions of a young, thin, muscular, and darkly complected man giving her flowers and a box of chocolates. I then saw the two of them making passionate love. This vision gave way to another scene where Tanya was marrying a totally different man. Her groom was tall and hunky. He looked as if he could have been an NFL Linebacker. They said their "I do's," and he picked her straight up in the air and planted a long, passionate kiss on her lips. I asked when this would take place and was told that she would meet her husband when her current lover broke her heart. I told Tanya what I had seen and heard.

She said, "Oh my God! The first man you described is the man I'm seeing now. Are you sure he's not the one? I have been seeing him for over a year now, and I feel that we are ready to take it to the next level. He has been hinting about getting married. I think that he may have already purchased my ring, but I don't know for sure. We were in the jewelry store one month ago, and I tried on engagement rings. He just has to propose to me soon. Are you sure that it's the second man that I am going to marry and not the first one?"

I told Tanya it was my job to tell her what I was seeing, hearing, and feeling from Spirit.

At the end of the reading, she stood up, smiled, gave me a hug, and stated, "You certainly described my current boyfriend. I just hope you're wrong about him not being the one."

One month later, Tanya called me. She was very upset and crying. Through her sobs, she said, "You were right.

It's over; he broke up with me. When am I supposed to meet the man who is going to be my husband?"

Referring to our earlier reading, I reminded her that Spirit said he would come into her life after the one she was with broke her heart. I told her that her future husband could come into her life at any moment and to just be open to the possibilities. I emphasized the wonderful love she was going to have with him and told her that although her heart was breaking now, Spirit had to create the space necessary for her true love to come into her life.

She stopped crying, took a deep breath, and said, "Tell Spirit that I'm ready for him to come now!"

I chuckled and told her I didn't have to tell Spirit anything because The Great Spirit had heard her heart a long time ago.

I Don't Have A German Grandmother!

Unfortunately, not everyone that I read is a true believer in spirit communication. That's okay. I appreciate a healthy dose of skepticism. I also think it's important for a client to remain objective and not believe everything that a medium or psychic might say, but to take everything he or she says with a grain of salt while maintaining an open mind. Psychics and mediums are not all created equal. Some may be very gifted, while others may not have any true gifts at all. Also, at times, even the best psychics and mediums have days where they either can't connect or have more misses than hits.

On this particular day, like most days, I had an excellent

connection with Spirit. It was a Saturday, and I was working the BMSE (Body, Mind, and Spirit Expo) in a large city on the east coast. By mid-afternoon, a lovely young college student with blonde hair and blue eyes sat in my chair. The reading went extremely well until her German grandmother came through to give her a message. Her grandmother showed me a scene where she was a young woman participating in exercise along with a larger group of other girls. She was wearing a sleeveless white cotton blouse and loose-fitting beige khaki shorts. She was a slender 5'4", woman with shoulder-length blonde hair and blue eyes. Her skin was flawless, and her complexion was very pale. She told me that she was part of a national girls' fitness effort because Germans were encouraged to be healthy and fit. She told me to tell her granddaughter that she was very proud of her and that she was sorry she couldn't be part of her life.

My young client became visibly agitated and proclaimed, "I don't have a German grandmother!"

I suggested she might want to ask her mother about the German grandmother when she went home that weekend. She stood up, took the card that she had taken from my card holder earlier, and tore it into two pieces. She walked over to the waste receptacle and threw the pieces into the trash. I thought to myself that it was a shame that she couldn't be open-minded enough to receive the message.

On the following Monday morning, I visited a metaphysical shop where I occasionally shopped but never gave readings. As soon as I walked in, one of the regular store clerks ran over to me from behind the counter and exclaimed:

> *I am so glad to see you! What are the odds that you would walk into the store this morning just ten minutes after a girl called looking for you? She said you gave her a reading on Saturday and told her she had a German grandmother. She said she went home this past weekend and asked her mother if she had a German Grandmother. After some hesitation, she said that her mother did confirm that she had a German Grandmother who had passed away in Germany a long time before she was born. It was her father's mother, and he preferred not to talk about her because she sent him away to live with his father in America when he was a small child. You see, his mother became pregnant by his G.I. father during WWII. However, his father was engaged to marry a woman back in the U.S., so there was no way he could have entertained the idea of marrying her and bringing her back to the States. A couple of years after the German mother gave birth to their son, she was finally able to track down the address of her American G.I. She sent him a letter letting him know they had a son together and she would not be able to care for him much longer because she was sick with cancer. The letter made its way into the hands of the G.I.'s wife, who wasted no time confronting her husband about his illegitimate son. In spite of her hurt and humiliation, she was able to rise above the situation and actually embrace it. In the two years that they had been married, she had not been able to conceive a baby. She*

saw this child as an opportunity to experience motherhood and to do the right thing for everyone involved. So, she lovingly told her husband to write back as quickly as possible to let the German mother know that they would gladly welcome her son into their lives and treat him as their own child. They wired money for travel expenses, and within a month, their new son had arrived on American soil. He quickly assimilated into the family and the American way of life. It didn't take long for their new two-year-old son, who spoke only German, to become fluent in English. Two years later, the American G.I. and his wife gave birth to a child of their own, a little girl. However, they always made sure that their German son knew he was their son and made no distinction between him and their other children. The German mother would not be spoken of again until his father made a deathbed confession. This confession made no difference to the German-born son because he had known no other mother but his American mother, and that was all he cared about. So he chose not to talk about it again or openly acknowledge his German mother. That is why his daughter never knew about her German grandmother.

I called this young granddaughter of German descent back later that Monday afternoon. She told me she wanted to finish the reading. I told her we had finished the reading, and there was really nothing more that her grandmother needed to say. Also, during this time, I was working on finishing my second Master's Degree, and I really didn't have more time to give. This story really demonstrates why it's so important to keep an open mind when receiving a reading. If something doesn't resonate with you during a reading, then it might make a lot of sense later on once you've received all of the facts.

We Made Kissy Faces

Sometimes a spirit will compel me to exhibit a certain gesture or mannerism they frequently displayed in life. For example, I gave a reading to Donna, the young mother of a 21-year-old gay man named Donovan who had committed suicide a year earlier. He and his mother made "kissy faces" to each other on a daily basis when he was still living at home before going off to college. The first thing I was compelled to do when I started channeling this young man was make kissy faces at his mother. I told her that I felt compelled to make a gesture, and I didn't want her to be offended or take it the wrong way. She said she thought she might know what I was talking about and said it was okay—she wouldn't be offended. When I started making kissy faces, she began to sob uncontrollably and said:

> *My son, Donovan, and I used to make kissy faces to each other every day. He was my only child. I never knew that my son was gay until he said so in his suicide note. I raised him in the Catholic faith. He was an altar boy for many years. I feel he killed himself because he couldn't deal with the guilt of being a homosexual, but I don't know for sure. Had I known then that he was gay, I would*

have told him that God loves and accepts him regardless of his sexual orientation. Maybe if he had been taught about the true love of God, he wouldn't have killed himself. I would have also told him that no religion is perfect, and no one knows exactly what God is. I have to know that my son is okay, that he is not suffering or in a bad place. That's why I'm here today. Please tell me whether or not he's in a good place, and if he's not, please help him get to a good place.

Her son spoke to me and said:

Tell my mom that she was the most wonderful mother anyone could ever have. She did everything right. I take full responsibility for ending my own life. I didn't kill myself because I was gay. I killed myself because I was depressed. My boyfriend, Chuck, to whom I was becoming very close, ended the relationship with me. I walked in and caught him making love with someone else in his dorm room. I really felt Chuck was the love of my life, and I would never find anyone I could love as much as him. I was hoping we would stay together and eventually get married. When he broke up with me, he told me that I should probably get tested for HIV. I think he made this comment just to be hurtful. I was also being bullied at school and failing most of my college classes. The professors weren't very helpful or supportive either. I just couldn't take dealing with life anymore. Please tell her I did what I felt was the best thing to do at the time, and there was nothing anyone could have done to prevent it.

I take full responsibility for my death, and I am at peace. I want her to be at peace too. I have been with her since my death. I have seen glimpses of the light, and I can feel the warm, unconditional love of God that my mother was talking about. Let her know that you will cross me over into heaven and that I will watch over her from there.

I told Donna what he had just said to me about being depressed and taking full responsibility for ending his life—that he was at peace and wanted her to be at peace too. I also told her he was still earthbound because he had stayed with her since the time of his death, but I would be crossing him over into Heaven that evening.

Through her tears, Donna said, "I still can't help but feel that I am somehow partially responsible for his death."

I reminded her about what her son had said in his message—that he takes full responsibility for his death; he's at peace, and he wants her to be at peace too.

She sighed deeply, and I gave her a kissy face. She smiled and gave me a kissy face and a hug. I crossed her son over that evening. It was a joyous crossing with beautiful angels and ancestors to greet him in the loving presence of the Creator.

If you know someone in the LGBTQ community who is severely depressed and showing signs of suicidal ideations or tendencies, please help them seek help or get help for them. The LGBTQ community may be disproportionately at-risk for suicidal feelings and other mental health struggles because of the discrimination and prejudice they so frequently encounter. At the time of this writing, the suicide prevention lifeline is 1-800-273-8255, or visit their website at *https://suicidepreventionlifeline.org/help-yourself/lgbtq/*.

The Sweet Spirit Of Roscoe The Dog

Not often do I channel someone's pet, but when I do, it can be heartbreaking and warming at the same time. A lady named Jennifer made an appointment with me in hopes of hearing from a loved one. She didn't say who the loved one was that she wanted to hear from, and I didn't ask because I never ask. The less I know upfront, the better I like it because Spirit is then able to validate much more information that the client knows is not coming from me. It's unusual for me to begin seeing animals when I first start reading. Usually, I will initially feel the way someone died, then see what they looked like, followed by their personality and ultimately their message.

During the opening of this reading, a beautiful black lab revealed himself to me. He was sitting on the right side of my client with a big smile on his face. He had a shiny coat and did not appear to be sick. I didn't feel any illness, as I normally do when I channel a human spirit. Instead, I saw what looked like a huge tumor, but it wasn't on the dog. I told my client that I saw a Black lab sitting on her right side. I also told her about the tumor that I saw and that it wasn't on the dog.

She smiled as tears flowed down her cheeks and said, "He's why I'm here. I wasn't sure if you'd be able to channel animals or not, but apparently, you can. His name was

Roscoe, and he died from cancer three months ago. I had to have him put to sleep."

I told her that I felt Roscoe was trying to tell me that he was no longer sick with cancer. He proceeded to show me a scene where he was running through a beautiful field of tall, green grass. In the vision, he stopped and looked down. Lying low in the grass was a huge litter of puppies of all breeds and colors.

Roscoe said, "These are my babies, and they will need a home soon. Please tell Jennifer that it's time to rescue a puppy like she rescued me. Because of her love, I had a full and happy life. It's time for her to be happy again. I am well and will always be with her from the other side until the time we are reunited in Heaven."

I shared with Jennifer the vision and message that Roscoe had just given me.

She began to sob, and through her tears, she said, "I've been thinking about getting another dog, but I just don't think that I could stand to lose another one. I miss Roscoe so much, I don't even know if another dog could fill the void."

I reminded her that Roscoe showed me puppies who would soon need a home and lots of love. I went on to tell her what I was hearing from Roscoe at that moment—that the decision to get another dog should not be based on the possibility of loss but on the love and wonderful life she could give to a very deserving little puppy. Jennifer stopped crying and stated emphatically that she would be visiting the dog pound that afternoon to get just the right dog. Jennifer called me several days later to let me know she had adopted two puppies, a golden retriever, and a yellow lab. She said she was so glad she had a reading with me and that she could feel Roscoe's spirit around her all of the time. She asked me what Roscoe thought about the two new puppies. I told her that Roscoe said he really liked the new puppies and would be watching over them to guide and protect.

~ Eleven ~

MY SCARIEST GHOST INVESTIGATIONS

The thing I find really scary about ghosts and demons is that you don't really know what they are or where they are...So it's the kind of thing you don't even know how to defend yourself against.
~ Oren Peli

The Spirit Of Sexual Perversion Of The Innocents

I was asked to come to the home of a client named Jeff to see if I could figure out what was causing disturbances in his newly built house. He had been to me for a reading a year earlier and said I was the first one he thought of contacting when he started having experiences in his home that he couldn't explain. He and his family had been living in the house for only six months when strange things started to happen. For instance, objects would disappear and reappear somewhere else in the house. Several times, Jeff placed his car keys in a bowl on the bureau in his bedroom before going to bed, only to find them on the kitchen table the next morning. Jeff also told me that he and his wife had been seeing an old man in the downstairs hallway as well as shadow people. He said that he could not understand why they would be having such experiences in a brand new house. Whatever was in the house was also disturbing his two toddlers. He said that the kids had not slept in their own beds for the last four months because of nightmares and complaints of monsters in their rooms. I informed Jeff that if he was experiencing some kind of haunting, it could be related to the land or a house that occupied the same space on the land as his house. Before hanging up, we agreed upon a date and time for me to come out and investigate.

During my phone conversation with Jeff, I started receiving impressions about his new home. For the next several days, up to and including the day of the investigation, I continued to receive impressions that were very disturbing. I kept seeing an old man taking pictures of young boys and girls in the nude and in various suggestive postures. I was shown how he lured them into his house by giving them candy and expensive gifts. He promised to give them more gifts each time they came to his house and played in their birthday suits. He said that they had to take all of their clothes off so that he could wash them because he didn't like any dirt in his house. He told them he wanted to take pictures of them while they played with their toys and each other so that he could show his family how happy he was with his new friends. He made them promise to keep their special friendship a secret, or their parents might keep them from getting more gifts. He also told them their parents didn't love them as much as he did, or they would let them do whatever they wanted to do and give them all of the toys that they wanted.

I knew that I had my work cut out for me on this investigation. On the day of the investigation, I received the impression of an empty, old, and dilapidated house being demolished to clear the land for a new house. The new house had apparently been built on the site of an old house, a house this perverted man had occupied before his death. I was also shown a scene where the old man was taken out of a prison cell in a body bag. Apparently, he had been arrested and brought to justice for his crimes of pornography involving innocent children. Now, the spirit of this old man was loose in the brand-new home of my client and his family. It was up to me to get him out so they could live in peace without interference from the demon in human form that I referred to as Mr. Pervert.

In the morning and evening of the investigation, I communed with The Great Spirit and commanded its help in the form of its mightiest warrior angel, St. Michael, the Archangel. I communicated my command to God by visualizing St. Michael leading thousands of his warrior angels to do battle against what I perceived as the Spirit of Sexual Perversion of the Innocents. I continued to watch while my creative visualization morphed into an observation. At that point, I knew God was manifesting the outcome I was seeking. The angels took hold of the evil spirit, binding it with rope while freeing the human soul it had possessed. I continued to watch as the angels escorted the old man into the light of The Creator and the evil spirit into the black abyss.

The word *abyss* means "a deep hole", so deep that it seems bottomless or immeasurable. It is often used in modern contexts to describe the bottomless sea. In the Bible and in Jewish theology, the Abyss is often a metaphorical reference to the place of evil spirits. Sometimes the Abyss is pictured as a deep or bottomless hole in the earth. According to my understanding, the abyss is a dark and cold place where all evil is destroyed and eventually transmuted into nothingness or neutral energy.

In the 1906 edition of the Jewish Encyclopedia, Mr. Kaufmann Kohler, Ph.D. (now deceased), cited the following usage of the word abyss as it occurs in both the old and new Testaments of the Bible (JewishEncyclopedia.com):

...the place of punishment of the wicked; hell; the abode of certain demons. As such, the Abyss of Fire is mentioned in the Book of Enoch (xviii. 11-16, 19; xxi. 1-6; xc. 21-25) as the prison-house of impure angels (compare Luke, viii. 31; Rev. ix. 1; xi. 7—Abyss, the seat of the dragon; xx. 3, where "Satan is cast into the abyss, shut up, and a seal set upon him"). According to the Prayer of Manasseh, verse 3, the Lord has closed and sealed up the Abyss by His awful and mystic name. There was a place beneath the altar of the Temple at Jerusalem believed to lead down to the very Abyss of the world, the foundation stone of the earth being placed there (Suk. 49a, 53a; see Targ. Yer. Ex. xxviii.

> *30, and Zohar, iii. 61). In the cosmography of the rabbis (Midr Konen), the Abyss forms part of Gehenna; it is beneath the ocean and consists of three, or seven, departments, one above the other. In the Cabala, the opening of the great Abyss in the lower world, sealed with the seal that bears the Holy Name, plays a great role as the seat of the evil spirits, and with it corresponds the opening of the great Abyss in the upper world as a cosmogonic element.*

All faiths seem to have either an underworld or some other realm where the dead go, even if they believe in reincarnation. Judeo-Christian faiths, including Muslims, are not the only religions that have a hellish abode. Buddhism also has a hell, but you have to be a pretty horrible person to go there.

Later that afternoon, I made sure that I had everything I felt I needed in my spirit removal and house blessing basket. The contents of my basket included the following items:

- White Sage

- Holy Water

- Holy Oil with extra virgin olive oil, frankincense, and myrrh

- Frankincense and Myrrh incense with a swinging incense burner

- Kosher Salt

- A booklet that I had made consisting of various Catholic, Jewish, Unity, and Native American prayers and blessings.

- An Exorcist's Manual (just in case the spirit tried to jump a living soul).

Armed with my basket and the palpable presence of God's warrior angels by my side, I was ready to do some serious housecleaning. We arrived at Jeff's home at six o'clock in the evening, as planned. It was summertime, so there was plenty of daylight left to accomplish what we needed to do. Jeff, along with his wife and two children, were standing at the entrance of the driveway. Once we were out of the car, I asked Jeff why everyone was standing outside. He told me that when they got home about an hour earlier, the house looked like a cyclone had hit it. There wasn't anything of value missing, so he knew that they hadn't been robbed. He said that it had to be a ghost or some kind of spirit. I told him that it would probably be a good idea to take his family to dinner at a nice restaurant followed by a funny movie at the theater while I conducted my investigation and cleansing. Jeff and his family quickly agreed to my suggestion. They didn't waste any time jumping into their car and taking off down the road.

I was definitely relieved that they would be taken out of harm's way in case the spirit in the house turned violent. Fortunately for me, my husband, Michael, was with me that evening, as he had been on just about all of my investigations up to that point. I knew that I had some much-needed support. I don't think I would have entered that house alone if he hadn't been with me. We cautiously entered the kitchen through the door from the garage. We were both awestruck by the condition of the kitchen. The refrigerator door was wide open. Milk, eggs, food, and condiments were splattered against the walls and floor. All the cabinets and drawers were open, with a few shards of broken glass and pottery on the floor and countertops. Navigating our way around the broken pieces of glass and pottery, we finally entered the dining room. It wasn't as bad as the kitchen. A couple of the dining room chairs were turned over on their sides. The doors to the china hutch were wide open, but everything inside was still intact and in place, with nothing broken. The downstairs bathroom appeared to be intact, with nothing out of place. In the living room, there were knick-knacks, books, and pillows strewn all over the floor. We entered the hallway from the living room and took the stairs to the second level. The stairs and second-level hallway were clear. Nothing seemed out of place until we opened the door to the master bedroom. All of the drawers in the bureau and chest of drawers were open, with clothes hanging out. I didn't think that clothes hanging out of the drawers were necessarily paranormal. That could be attributed to someone's personal housekeeping habits. When we walked over to the entrance of the master bathroom, however, I changed my mind. We stood there but didn't go in because there were copious amounts of what looked like hand lotion and shampoo smeared all over the floor and mirror. A roll of toilet paper had been unraveled and scattered over the toilet and bathtub. We walked out of the master bedroom and back into the hallway. The hall bathroom looked neat, clean, and undisturbed. The other two other bedrooms were in similar condition to the master bedroom—all of the clothes drawers were open with clothes hanging out and scattered all over the floor. The upstairs family room was neat and clean, with nothing out of place.

When we finished our tour of the house, we both commented on how we sensed we were being watched as we moved from room to room. I called on God and St. Michael the Archangel and then began cleansing the house while reciting prayers of protection. After I had completed my prayers, I started commanding the evil spirit, which I had discerned earlier as the Spirit of Sexual Perversion of the Innocents, to leave and go to where God had commanded it to go—to the Abyss. I also commanded the evil spirit to release the spirit of the old man. I told the old man to come out of the evil spirit and cross over into the light of heaven. The old man's spirit told me that he was not worthy. I told him he was worthy and would be cleansed from all wrongdoing and evil inclinations when he crossed over into God's unconditional love and light. In my mind's eye, I watched as he stepped into the light, never looking back. I also watched as the evil spirit spiraled endlessly into the bottomless pit. Once the old man's spirit was crossed over and the demon was cast into the abyss, I anointed each doorway and window by making the sign of the cross with holy oil over each one. After anointing the inside of the house, I went outside and put down a boundary line with kosher salt around the perimeter of the property.

To finish the property cleansing, blessing, and protection ritual, I buried St. Michael medallions in each corner of the yard.

We went back inside the house to wait for the client and his family to return home. About 15 minutes later, they drove into the driveway and stopped short of pulling into the garage. We walked outside, and I told Jeff and his wife we did a cleansing, blessing, and protection ritual, and nothing out of the ordinary happened. I also told them about the impressions and visualizations I had earlier that day. He asked me why the house looked like a cyclone had hit it. I told him I didn't know why, and the only thing I could figure was that when I visualized St. Michael binding the demon and casting it into the abyss earlier that day, it became enraged and showed its anger by throwing a temper tantrum and tearing the house apart. I told him that the soul of the old man had been released from the demon, and I had crossed him over into the light while St. Michael threw the evil spirit into the abyss. I informed him that I believed his home was clean and that it was safe for him and his family to live there. I asked him to let me know if they experienced anything unusual in the next few weeks.

A month later, I called Jeff to get a follow-up report to see if the activity had permanently stopped. He was very appreciative that I had called and said that nothing more had happened—everything was peaceful. I had another reading with him a couple of years later, and things were still quiet. This incident happened a long time ago, and as far as I know, everything has remained peaceful since then.

Hell House

I tried to keep my abilities a secret while on the job, but because of my compulsion to help others, my secret often leaked out. I was hired to work full-time on the Cardiac Step-down Unit at this hospital. The Cardiac Step-down Unit is a step down from the Cardiac Intensive Care Unit; however, on this particular day, I floated to the Medical-Surgical Unit. Being made to float to other units is not unusual for a hospital nurse. If needed, the nurses on our unit were often sent to a unit that was severely understaffed. No one really liked to float, but we all had to take turns. Other units were also required to float.

During my lunch break in the med-surg staff lounge, I overheard one of the travel nurses, Rebecca, talking about how she had just had a mammogram a week earlier that showed a one-centimeter lump in her left breast. She said she was scheduled to have a biopsy done the next day, and she didn't know how she was going to get through the rest of her workday without constantly crying. I immediately had a vision of three ladies dressed in colorful African-style clothing. They were also wearing headscarves. The lady in the middle said that she was the mother, and the ladies on each side of her were her sisters. She told me to please tell her daughter not to worry, that the lump would be benign and she would be okay. Also, remind her that both of my sisters and I had fibroids in our breasts, which were harmless. Since I was at work, I didn't want to convey the message, but when Rebecca started crying uncontrollably, I knew that I had to try and help by telling her about the vision and message I had just received.

As soon as we were alone in the break room, I walked over to her table and sat down beside her. I told her that while she was talking about her lump, I had a vision of three ladies wearing beautiful African-style clothing and head turbans. The one in the middle said that she was your mother, and the other two women with her were your aunts.

She stopped crying and looked up at me through her tears: "My mother had two sisters, and they were very close. They all passed away years ago."

I asked her if she would like to hear the message her mother gave me. She nodded her head and said yes. I told her what her mother had said to me—not to worry because the lump would be benign and she would be okay. Also, her mother and two sisters had fibroids in their breasts, which were harmless. Rebecca gasped and stated that I was right; she had a family history of fibrocystic breast disease.

She hugged my neck and told me that I was a Godsend. I asked her to please not tell anyone about what I did; I needed to keep my abilities a secret. She promised me that she wouldn't tell.

About a week and a half later, I discovered she didn't keep her promise. Karen, the nurse manager from that unit, approached me on my unit and said she had heard that I have special abilities. I told her I didn't know what she was talking about. She said it was okay. I wasn't in trouble. I told her I wasn't worried about being in trouble; I just didn't want everybody at work to know. I asked Karen how she came to know.

She said that Rebecca went to her office on the same day she received the message from her mother and told her that if her biopsy came back positive, she might have to have surgery and chemotherapy. That would mean that she would have to go on FMLA during her treatment. Rebecca also told her about the message I gave her from her mother—not to worry; the lump would be benign and she would be okay.

Karen went on to tell me she was both shocked and thankful to hear that my prediction was correct when Rebecca's biopsy results finally came back and showed that her cyst was benign. Karen also said she had been praying for someone who could provide spiritual help for her daughter, and she believed that I was the one.

Karen's daughter, Victoria, and her two children had been under some kind of supernatural attack for the past couple of months, ever since they moved into an old rental house in the country. Victoria had finally found a house that was affordable and spacious enough for her and her two daughters so that she could leave her abusive husband. This house was supposed to be their safe haven, but it turned out to be their worst nightmare. From the moment they moved in, they were plagued with supernatural occurrences such as lights and televisions going on and off, raps and knocking coming from the walls, and shadows in the hallway.

Victoria's oldest daughter was seeing a seven-foot shadow man standing at the foot of the bed during the night, while her youngest daughter was seeing and talking to a little girl ghost. Victoria had been having nightmares about a devilish-looking female dressed in black clothing with black hair and red, glowing eyes. This female always had three black Doberman Pinschers with her. These dogs also had red, glowing eyes. With drool dripping from their mouths, they bared their long canine teeth and growled as if they were ready to attack her. She said that all the supernatural activity was bad enough, but the straw that broke the camel's back occurred when she walked into the kitchen one morning to find all of the cabinet doors and drawers open with dishes and food strewn all over the floor.

I asked Karen if Victoria might have a rodent problem in the house. She said that Victoria's landlord just had the house inspected by an exterminator, and they didn't find anything. I asked her if it was possible that her granddaughters could have made the mess in the kitchen. She said absolutely not! Her granddaughters were very sweet and well-behaved children. I then asked her if there were any teenagers in the house. Karen said that Victoria's two daughters were ages six and seven, and Victoria was in her mid-thirties. I thought to myself, *Well, that rules out any poltergeist activity related to the children, but it's possible that Victoria could be a poltergeist agent.*

Current paranormal research suggests that a poltergeist agent is someone who is believed to have telekinetic ability and can move objects with the power of their mind. Although a poltergeist agent can be male or female of any age, the agent is usually either a teenage girl or a very young woman. Researchers have discovered that in many poltergeist cases, there are complex and emotionally conflicted family dynamics. Often, the family has a strict, authoritarian, and punitive regime and may be strongly religious. One widely accepted theory is that poltergeist phenomena are a psychokinetic manifestation of the agent's intense repressed anger at another, more powerful, and controlling family member. Sometimes the anger seems to be directed at oneself, so that the poltergeist agent becomes the victim.

Many parapsychologists continue to hold the traditional view that poltergeists are noisy spirits. According to Merriam-Webster online, a poltergeist is a noisy, usually mischievous ghost held to be responsible for unexplained noises such as rapping. After interviewing Karen and Victoria, I was under the impression that this incident had nothing to do with a poltergeist agent. I firmly believed then, as I do now, that the poltergeist activity in that house was the result of powerful entities.

Karen said things were so bad that for the last couple of weeks, her daughter and grandchildren had been staying with her. They haven't even gone back to their own house to get much-needed clothing. She said they were in crisis mode because she lived in a small, one-bedroom, one-bathroom house that was not meant for four people. She told me her daughter had signed a one-year lease for their rental house, and there was no way she could afford to break it. She pleaded with me to do what I could to cleanse her daughter's house. I told her I would do my best. She said that she would talk to her daughter, and they would be calling me soon to set up a time to meet at the house.

I worked three twelve-hour shifts per week, and I had already completed three shifts in a row, so I had the next few days off. I slept in until about eight o'clock the next morning and woke feeling rested and refreshed. I thought about what Karen had said the day before, and I knew I had to try to help them. After breakfast, I turned off the television and went into meditative prayer. I asked God to show me the truth about what was going on at Victoria's house. Immediately, I started having visions of the shadow people and the female demon, accompanied by three hellhounds with glowing, red eyes and sharp, canine teeth. Several shadow people roamed the hallways, and one giant shadow man stayed in the back bedroom. I was told of a portal in the center of the hallway where spirits could come and go from the underworld as they wanted. I was further told that the female demon with her three hellhounds represented the gates of hell and conveyed the message that an entrance to hell was in the house. I was also shown a young man dressed in black robes in the act of conjuring evil spirits. He appeared to be performing some type of black mass ritual. It immediately occurred to me that he was the reason that a portal to hell existed in that house. This black ceremonial magician was responsible for the creation of the portal.

All of a sudden, I felt overwhelmed and unsure that I would be able to help Victoria and her family. My initial impulse was to tell her to forget about living in that house and to just ride out the storm by staying with her mother until she could get another place. I had never encountered anything like this in my life. If I was going to do this cleansing, I knew that I needed the help of the clergy. I felt it would not be wise for me to do this alone. There is strength in numbers, and I was determined to help Victoria and her daughters by getting an army of light workers and clergy if I needed to.

I immediately started looking for priests and pastors in the area who would be able and willing to work with me. I looked for two weeks and couldn't find anyone to help. I would have to cleanse this property and close the portal on my own. My husband, Michael, was not versed in spiritual matters, but he was always ready to lend me his support. I took a week to prepare myself spiritually for the upcoming battle against the dark forces in that house. I prepared by feeding my mind and soul with positive affirmations and faith-filled scriptures such as:

> *Many are the afflictions of the righteous, but the Lord delivers him out of them all. (Psalm 34:19)*
>
> *He will cover you with his pinions, and under his wings you will find refuge; his faithfulness is a shield and buckler. (Psalm 91:4)*
>
> *The Lord will keep you from all evil; he will keep your life. The Lord will keep you going out and coming in from this time forth and forevermore. (Psalm 121:7-8)*

> *Though I walk in the midst of trouble, you preserve my life; you stretch out your hand against the wrath of my enemies, and your right hand delivers me. (Psalm 138:7)*

By the end of the week, I felt ready to do battle. However, I was still very apprehensive about dealing with what was in that house, but I knew it had to be done. Three weeks after my initial conversation with Karen, I finally had a scheduled date and time to meet with both Karen and Victoria to investigate and cleanse the house. For the next two nights, I had frightening dreams that involved exhausting battles with demons. I would wake up shaken, but I did not let that discourage me because, in my dreams, I defeated the demons every time! Three days later, when the day of the anticipated battle finally arrived, I was confident and ready to cleanse Victoria's house of its resident evil and close the portal. I proceeded pretty much the same way as I had in my last cleansing, where I had the demon evicted from the house. I visualized St. Michael the Archangel and his legions of angels binding and casting the female demon, the hellhounds, and all the evil spirits back through the portal to hell, where they came from. I then watched as St. Michael closed and sealed the portal so that it could never be opened again.

As soon as I had packed my house cleansing and blessing basket, I didn't waste any time getting out the door. Victoria's house was over an hour's drive in the country. It was a beautiful, sunny spring afternoon with a temperature of about 74 degrees and a gentle breeze that carried the scent of blooming dogwood trees and jasmine through the air. As we traveled down the country roads, I couldn't imagine how evil could exist anywhere on such a beautiful planet. I thought to myself that *the Creator intended the earth to be a very good place.* As I pondered the thought, I asked the Creator why evil exists. Of course, I didn't get a clear answer to that question. What I did receive in response to my inquiry was that it was up to people like me to try to eradicate as much evil as possible.

Within what seemed like no time, we were pulling into Victoria's driveway. There wasn't a garage, and there were no other cars in the driveway. We checked the address to make sure we were at the right house, and apparently, we were. Within a couple of minutes, Karen pulled into the driveway behind us. She apologized for being a few minutes late. She said that she wanted to be sure that we got there before they did because she didn't want to go anywhere near the house without someone there to protect them. As we walked up the driveway towards the side entrance of the red brick, ranch-style house, we were all somewhat unnerved by the cacophony of howling and baying dogs in the deep woods behind the house. Normally, howling dogs in the country would be no big deal; however, because of the nature of the haunting, it felt somewhat ominous.

Before entering the house, I suggested that we say a few prayers of protection. We stood in a circle and held each other's hands while I led us in every prayer of protection that I could think of. The following prayers are the ones I recall using that day:

The Light of God surrounds us.

The Love of God enfolds us.

The Power of God protects us.

The Presence of God watches over us.

Wherever we are, God Is, and all is well! (Unity Prayer)

Saint Michael the Archangel, defend us in battle.

Be our protection against the wickedness and snares of the devil.

May God rebuke him, we humbly pray;

and do Thou, O Prince of the Heavenly Host,

by the Divine Power of God,

cast into hell Satan and all the evil spirits

who roam throughout the world seeking the ruin of souls. (Catholic Prayer)

Because thou hast made the LORD, which is my refuge, even the Most High, thy habitation;

There shall no evil befall thee, neither shall any plague come nigh thy dwelling.

For he shall give his angels charge over thee, to keep thee in all thy ways.

They shall bear thee up in their hands, lest thou dash thy foot against a stone.

Thou shalt tread upon the lion and the adder: the young lion and the dragon shalt thou trample under feet. (Psalm 91:9-13).

Many are the afflictions of the righteous, but the Lord delivers him out of them all (Psalm 34:19).

The Lord will keep you from all evil; he will keep your life. The Lord will keep your going out and your coming in from this time forth and forevermore (Psalm 121:7-8).

Though I walk in the midst of trouble, you preserve my life; you stretch out your hand against the wrath of my enemies, and your right hand delivers me (Psalm 138:7).

But the Lord is faithful, and he will strengthen you and protect you from the evil one (2 Thessalonians 3:3).

We entered the house one by one, with me leading the procession. Other than the musky odor, no doubt the result of a closed-up house, nothing seemed out of the ordinary. The kitchen was brightly lit, with the sun beaming through the two kitchen windows over the sink. The yellow chiffon paint on the walls added a pleasant and welcoming feel. I initially sensed that this room would be a nice place to sit, have a cup of tea, and read a good book. It wasn't long before that illusion was shattered. No sooner had we all made our way out of the kitchen and halfway down the hall, we heard the sound of crashing dishes and doors slamming. We turned around and walked back into the kitchen, just standing there in awe with our mouths dropped open. The cabinet doors were swinging wildly, slamming shut and quickly opening again. Dishes were being thrown out of the cabinets and scattered all over the floor. Ceramic canisters containing flour, sugar, and coffee that were sitting on the countertop were turned over and the contents poured out onto the countertop and floor. I could not believe my eyes. If I hadn't seen this activity while it was happening, I probably would have speculated that maybe Victoria had rats in her cabinets, and I would have been looking for droppings. But I did see it with my own eyes, and so did everyone else. There was no denying that they had a big problem, and it definitely wasn't a rat infestation. A very powerful spirit had to be the cause of this poltergeist activity.

We all stood there for several minutes, trying to make sense of what had just happened. I could feel the level of fear starting to rise in that room to the point where it was almost palpable. The incessant barking of dogs coming from the woods behind the house didn't help matters either. We all wanted to run out and never go back. I told Karen and Victoria it was okay for them to wait outside if they wanted to and not to worry about trying to clean the kitchen up. They didn't waste any time getting out the door. Victoria stated while she was running out the door that she didn't care about anything in that house and that she wasn't going to stay there long enough to clean anything up either.

With Karen and Victoria out of the house, we started spiritually cleansing the kitchen. Michael placed the frankincense and myrrh incense into the incense diffuser and lit it. He began swinging it in every direction, making sure smoke filled the entire room. I started commanding the evil spirits in that house to return to the portal. As I made my commands, Michael read aloud prayers of protection, especially the St. Michael prayer.

Before we entered the hallway, I anointed the entrance with holy water by making the sign of the cross. We noticed an intense chill in the air as we entered. This hallway was centered in the middle of the house and led to all three bedrooms and a full bathroom. About halfway down the hall, we felt an intense blast of very cold, arctic-like air that chilled us to the bone. We looked around for any possible source of the cold—there weren't any vents in this hallway other than a return vent at the far end. The return vent filtered the air back to the ventilation system, not away from it, so it wasn't producing cold air. Then I realized that we had just walked across the portal to hell.

Michael and I continued down the hallway until we reached the very last bedroom on the far left. This was the room where Victoria's oldest daughter experienced the shadow man at the foot of her bed every night. Upon entering her room, I didn't notice anything unusual. However, as soon as I opened the bi-fold closet doors, I encountered a foul odor and a small, black, vaporous-looking mass that rushed by me. I thoroughly investigated the closet, looking for the source of the rotten smell. There was nothing in that closet but a few clothes hanging on racks. There were no shoes, storage boxes, or dirty clothes. I then knew that the foul smell was associated with the black mass. I called out to the foul spirit and commanded it to go to the abyss through the portal. I visualized St. Michael binding and casting the tall shadow man into the blackness of hell through the portal. After the visualization, I noticed that the smell was completely gone.

In the bedroom of the youngest daughter, I encountered an evil spirit that presented itself as a blonde-haired, blue-eyed little girl. I knew it was evil because of the way it made me feel—as if it were a cunning predator. It only wanted one thing—to gain the trust of Victoria's little girl and possess her soul. I told this entity I knew it was a deceitful spirit looking to possess the soul of child. I commanded it to return to hell through the portal. In my mind's eye, I watched as St. Michael tossed this spirit into the abyss.

The master bedroom had a peculiar feel to it—as if it were command central for the demon in charge. This spirit was pervasive and controlled all of the other entities in the house and those that came through the portal. However, it did not interact directly with the living. It commanded lower-level demons to do its bidding. I could feel its hatred for me, and it tried to threaten me by making me feel afraid of its power. I didn't buy into these feelings. Instead, I stated my commands and recited my prayers.

Telepathically, I told this spirit that, by the power of God, St. Michael the Archangel was the head spirit in charge now, and he was going to toss her back into the abyss. I walked out of that bedroom knowing that I didn't have to challenge this demon in any way because St. Michael was already on the job.

When we entered the hall bathroom, the water faucets turned on in the shower and in the sink. The spirit's attempt to create fear in us did not work. I continued to command all the evil spirits in that house to go back through the portal to hell. We turned off all the water faucets, returned to the hallway, and proceeded to the living room. That was the only room left to cleanse. At this point, the house was filled with heavy smoke from the incense burner, and we could barely breathe. We knew that we had to finish soon and get out. As we entered the living room, the television turned on and off several times. Undaunted, I continued with the commands and visualizations while my husband continued swinging the incense burner and stating the prayers of protection.

If there were any spirits hiding in the house, they would have to be in the living room because I had anointed the doorpost of every room we had just cleansed with holy water by making the sign of the cross. They definitely weren't going to cross the threshold of an anointed and sealed room. As the television and the lamps blinked on and off, I continued stating my commands until the activity stopped and then I anointed the doors and windows in that room. Michael and I went back to the entrance of the hallway, where I visualized St. Michael closing up the portal. At the conclusion of my visualization, the house was eerily quiet. We could detect absolutely no activity. We walked to the center of the hallway, where we had previously experienced the intensely cold blast of air; it was no longer there. The temperature in this part of the hallway felt the same as the rest of the hallway. We walked back to the kitchen and picked up my basket. Then we walked out of the house through the side entrance from the kitchen. We found Karen and Victoria in the car at the end of the driveway. Victoria said they had thought about leaving but didn't because they were worried about us. Karen said they could see the television and lights going on and off through the living room windows the whole time we were in the house. I told both of them I believed the house was clean and that the portal was closed, but I didn't think it would be wise for Victoria to live there with her daughters. I told Karen I felt it would be best for her daughter and granddaughters to stay with her. She said she loved her family, and there was no way she was going to let them go back into that hell house.

A few days later, I received a thank-you card with a gift certificate to a nice steak restaurant. My husband and I enjoyed a delicious meal that evening. I initially expected some type of retaliation from the spirit world after the cleansing, but there was nothing. I slept well every night without any bad dreams. Karen reported that no one had experienced any fallout from the cleansing either and that they were all happy and healthy. The last I heard from Karen, Victoria started dating and met a wonderful man whom she married shortly after her divorce from her abusive husband. I often wonder about the people who have lived in that hell house since the cleansing. Have they experienced anything unusual? I hope not. I am keeping faith that the portal is closed and that it stays that way.

Sex Beyond The Grave

Belle was a beautiful lady in her early thirties with black hair, brown eyes, and an olive complexion. She was married to a computer programmer named Dennis, whom she said absolutely loved and adored her. They had no children together, but she had two children from her previous marriage. That marriage ended with the unexpected death of her husband, Alex, who had died tragically in a construction accident. I first met Belle three years earlier, when she came to me for a reading. At that time, she was hoping to hear from an aunt who was bipolar and had committed suicide as a way to escape her mental illness. Her aunt came through that day in a very emotional reading that contained a wonderful message of healing.

At the time Belle had her first reading with me, she probably would have never imagined that her husband would be dead a year later. Because her first reading with me was so successful, she decided to call me for another reading when her dead husband started having sex with her on a nightly basis. During the phone call, I asked Belle why she thought the entity was her husband and not something or someone else. She said that she knew it was Alex because the entity smelled like his favorite aftershave—Old Spice. She started to cry and said that the sex felt as it did when he was alive—that the size of the entity's manhood was unmistakably that of her dead husband—both the girth and the length.

She went on to say she didn't know how much longer she was going to be able to hide her secret from Dennis. She said Alex had been dead for two years, and she couldn't understand why he would be coming to her now that she had finally moved on with her life. She also told me that, about a month after Alex died, she had used an Ouija board to try and contact him but wasn't successful. She said she tried to communicate with him through the board on three different occasions but finally gave up on the last attempt when he still failed to come through. She told me she felt the reason he didn't come through was that he had moved on with his soul journey and was not interested in making contact with her.

I told Belle that even though she may not have been aware of her contact with Alex through the ouija, she had definitely opened up a portal for him to come into her life. She said she had considered trying to use the ouija again to talk to him when the sexual encounters first started. I warned her not to go anywhere near that board. I also told her not to destroy it because we would have to close the portal and permanently remove the ouija from her home. She agreed that she wouldn't go near the board again.

A week after my phone conversation with Belle, she came to my house at about nine o'clock in the morning after she had sent her children off to school. This was one of the most disturbing readings I have ever given. Alex didn't waste any time. As soon as we sat down at the table, he began to channel through me. He tried to compel me to hug Belle and give her a French kiss. I told him that I would absolutely not hug or kiss her. As the reading progressed, it became obvious to me that Alex had not accepted his death and was not willing to let go of Belle and cross over. He was invading her dreams and raping her on a nightly basis. I was extremely concerned about this unhealthy situation.

When I told Alex to back off, he became childlike, saying, "I'm so sorry. It's just because I love her so much and I want to be with her."

I told him that was no longer possible. I reminded him that he no longer had a physical body, and what he was perceiving as a body was actually an ethereal body with no real substance.

He said, "I don't care what kind of body I have. I am going to make love to my wife. Tell her that I will never let her go. She is mine, and I will love her for all eternity. I will not allow anyone to separate us, not ever! We are still married, and I am her husband, not that man who is living with her."

I told Alex that the man living with her was her husband in the eyes of God and the Law. I informed him that he had to cross over and that he didn't have any choice. I told him his physical life was over and the angels would be coming soon to escort him to the other side so he could be with relatives that had crossed over into the light.

He said, "I don't want to be with them. My father is probably in hell, and I am not going there to be with him.

My mother is in heaven, but I'm not good enough to be there with her."

I told him that everyone who goes to heaven enters by grace, and it is not possible to earn your way there. You get to heaven by being willing to go.

He said to me, "Lady, I told you that I'm not going. I will go when it's time for Belle to die, and we can go to heaven together."

I told him he was being selfish and that he had no right to interfere in Belle's life. I also told him he was violating a spiritual law that might have adverse consequences for him.

He said, "I don't care. I'm not leaving. If anybody leaves, I'll make sure it's that man who's sleeping in the bed with my wife, even if I have to kill him. Please tell her what I said."

I told Alex that I was not through dealing with him and that I was going to personally see to it that he got crossed over.

I took several deep breaths in preparation for delivering her dead husband's message. I prefaced the message by telling her I would do all I could to help her in this situation with Alex. I told her he had not crossed over, and he refused to go. I also told her Alex tried to jump me so that he could use my body to hug and kiss her. I conveyed a condensed and paraphrased version of Alex's message. In a nutshell, I told Belle that Alex was violating her just as she suspected and that he refused to let go of her. I warned her that she and her husband, Dennis, might be in danger because Alex said he was going to wait for her to die before he crossed over, and if he had to, he would kill Dennis to get him away from her. I also told Belle I believed she needed to have an exorcism because Alex was attached to her. Her house would also need to be cleansed and blessed. Any items that belonged to Alex would have to be permanently removed.

Belle looked at me through tearful eyes and said with determination, "I will do whatever it takes to get rid of Alex. I love Dennis, and I don't want to jeopardize his life or mine. I want us to have a wonderful, long life together. If Alex can physically touch me the way he does, then there's no telling what else he could possibly do."

I reassured Belle that I would do whatever I could to help. I told her that one of the first things we needed to do was find a priest or a deliverance minister. I asked her if she was holding on to anything that had belonged to Alex. She said that she did have a box of things that had belonged to him, such as his compass, pocket knife, a few pieces of clothing, and other odds and ends. She said she also had pictures of him and the family. I asked her why she wanted to hang onto some of his stuff. She said she wanted to be able to give these things to her children when they were older. I told her Alex's things, including the pictures, would have to be put into a box and sealed. I told her that once the container was sealed, it would have to be exorcised of his energy and blessed and that the seal must remain intact until after her death. I advised her to store Alex's stuff at a storage site away from her home after it had been sealed and cleansed. I reminded her not to let her children have the box until after her death. I told her that we would also have to cleanse her home in addition to sealing Alex's stuff and performing her deliverance. Once again, she said she would do whatever she had to to get rid of Alex's ghost.

After the reading, we both enjoyed a cappuccino and some chocolate almond biscotti. While we were snacking, I asked her if there was a specific priest or minister she wanted to use in her deliverance. She said she didn't have a priest or a minister, and she trusted my judgment to get the right person. I told her that I would start looking right away for someone in the clergy who could help. We talked for a while about her children and how they were doing in school with their studies and extracurricular activities. When we had finished our second cup of cappuccino, Belle stood up and, with tears in her eyes, gave me a big hug. She said she would love to stay longer, but she needed to get home and seal up Alex's things. I gave her a roll of duct tape and told her that it should be more than adequate to seal up his box of belongings. I told her I felt duct tape was the most appropriate tape to use because it was very tenacious and would be more difficult to remove than other tapes. She took the tape and gave me another hug before scurrying out the door.

As soon as she left, I started googling for clergy people who specialize in deliverance. Within two hours, I found a preacher named Juanita who was willing to work with a medium. I explained to her that Belle had tried to contact her dead husband through an Ouija board after he died, which I believed opened a portal for him to come through and attach to her. I told the preacher that Belle's dead husband was sexually violating her every night and had also threatened to kill her current husband. Juanita said she would be available only for the next few days, and then she would be traveling to other churches to hold revival services. I told Juanita I would call Belle and then call her right back.

After hanging up with the preacher. I immediately called Belle and told her that I had found a deliverance minister who was willing to help us cross Alex over, but she would only be available for the next few days, so we had to act quickly. She said any of those days would work for her, but sooner would be better than later, so we should do it the next morning. I told her that worked for me, and I would call Juanita back and let her know we were on for the next morning. She also told me she had placed all of Alex's belongings and pictures in a plastic container and sealed it with the tape I gave her. I told her that was awesome, and I would cleanse and bless the container the next morning. Before getting off the phone with her, I made sure she understood that it was okay for her to call me if she needed to. I called Juanita back as soon as I got off the phone with Belle and made arrangements for us to meet at Belle's house the next morning at nine o'clock.

I slept well that night after doing my bedtime meditation and affirmations. I fell asleep, visualizing St. Michael the Archangel and his angels keeping charge over Belle so that she would remain safe and rest well that night. I arose bright and early at seven o'clock the next morning. The sun streamed brightly through my bedroom windows while a chorus of birds who made their home in the oak trees behind my house sang a sweet song. I quickly dressed and ran downstairs to make myself a high-protein breakfast consisting of scrambled eggs and lean beef sausage with toast and coffee. I was out the front door by eight o'clock and headed over to Belle's house, which was thirty minutes away with morning traffic.

Pastor Juanita had already arrived and was waiting in her car on the side of the road by the time I got there. I pulled in behind her, got out of my car, and walked toward hers. As I approached, I noticed that she was reading her Bible, no doubt preparing for the possible battle that lay ahead. When she saw me approaching, she got out of her car to greet me. We shook hands and formally introduced ourselves to each other. I asked her how she felt and what her perceptions were about what lay ahead of us. She said she could already feel some resistance from the attached spirit, but she had prayed and meditated on scriptures all morning long and was ready to do battle. She said she could feel the presence of the Holy Spirit within her, and she knew we already had the victory. We walked up the sidewalk leading to Belle's house together and knocked on the front door. Belle didn't waste any time letting us in, and she seemed to be in a very good mood. She offered us coffee and some breakfast danishes, but Juanita declined and said that she was ready to get started.

Juanita asked Belle where the most comfortable and relaxing space in the house was so that we could proceed with the deliverance session. Belle led us into a well-furnished and decorated sunroom with a gorgeous view of her gardens. She had vegetable, flower, and rose gardens filled with colorful and beautiful plants. I asked Juanita if it would be okay if I left the house while she was performing the deliverance or if I should stay with her. She said that I should stay with her and that we could both cleanse and bless the house afterward. I agreed that it was a good idea to work together, so I stayed with her.

Juanita had Belle recline comfortably on the sofa. Belle became extremely agitated as soon as Juanita anointed her with Holy Water, put the pastoral sash on her chest, and began saying prayers. About fifteen seconds into the deliverance, Belle's voice changed and became much deeper. She let out a low-pitched growl like a dog and then screamed for us to stop hurting her and to get out. Her body writhed in pain as if she were a worm in hot ashes. She started hurling profanities at the two of us. The sash that Juanita had placed on Belle's chest seemed to act as some sort of restraint that kept Belle from coming off the couch and attacking us. We were in no way physically binding Belle or holding her down. It was as if the sash were imbued with some sort of invisible power capable of restraining evil. Juanita continued to say prayers while ordering the attached spirit to leave and go where God commanded it to go. At the same time, I visualized St. Michael taking hold of the spirit of Alex and escorting it to heaven.

About thirty minutes into the session, Belle started coughing and gagging, so I immediately found a waste basket that she could vomit into. Anyone who participates in deliverance rituals knows that one of the first signs of depossession occurs when the victim starts vomiting. It is possible, however, for a possessing spirit to try to fool the deliverers, so we were cautious. Juanita continued to say prayers for at least fifteen minutes after Belle stopped vomiting. She was no longer writhing, cussing, or screaming for us to stop and get out. She was now crying and thanking us for helping her. She said that she no longer felt a weight on her chest or pressure in her back as she did during the deliverance. She sat up on the side of the sofa, and through her tears, she thanked us incessantly. Juanita asked Belle if she would be willing to partake in the Eucharist as a symbol of her acceptance of Christ, who had delivered her. Belle agreed, so Juanita provided her with Holy Communion. I believe that her willingness and ability to take communion were the litmus tests I felt we needed to make sure Alex had crossed over and was really gone.

When Belle had recovered from her ordeal, she accompanied us throughout the house, helping us to cleanse and bless it. I asked her where she had put Alex's things. She led us to the garage and opened the door. She pointed to a shelf on the far side of the garage and said it was the blue container marked "A's stuff." Juanita followed me over to the container, while Belle stayed behind at the door. Juanita anointed the plastic box with holy water and decreed it to be clean by the blood of the Lamb of God. Lastly, we cleansed and blessed the garage and the car that was parked there.

I asked Belle where she kept the Ouija board. She led us to the downstairs hall closet, where she had stored it on the highest shelf. She opened the door and pointed to it, saying, "I've been warned. I'm not going anywhere near that dreadful thing." I reached in and retrieved it. Belle and Juanita followed me into the kitchen, where I placed the box on the table. I opened it up and took the board and planchette out. Juanita immediately anointed it with holy oil. I commanded that all spirits that came through the portal be returned to the spirit world through the portal, especially the spirit of Alex. I called upon St. Michael the Archangel to escort all spirits back through the portal of the board, and I watched as St. Michael did so. I moved the planchette to goodbye and announced that the board was officially closed. Juanita commanded the board to be closed in the name of Jesus and sealed by the blood of the Lamb.

The deliverance, cleansing, and blessing took four hours. Belle asked us if we would join her for lunch. She said she wanted to show her appreciation for what we did for her. Juanita thanked Belle for her offer but said she really needed to be going so that she could get started on her to-do list before going out of town. Juanita did not ask for money, but Belle wrote her a check for a significant amount.

I told Belle I would definitely take her up on her offer for lunch, and after Juanita left, we agreed on a nice restaurant about ten minutes away. We took separate cars and met there. I took the Ouija board with the intent of disposing of it properly. Now that the portal in the board was closed, I could safely burn it, which I did later that evening.

Lunch was pleasant and uneventful. During lunch, I

told Belle I believed she was definitely free and that Alex had crossed over and would not be able to hurt her from the other side. I told her to call me if she or her family members experienced anything out of the ordinary. After lunch, we said our goodbyes, with no plans to follow up with one another. A week later, I received a beautiful thank-you note through the mail from Belle. It included a sizable gift certificate to a local day spa. On the card, she stated that she had been sleeping soundly every night with no sign of Alex. The last time I heard from Belle, her husband, Dennis, had accepted a promotion that took them to Colorado.

EPILOGUE

As I reflect on my scariest investigations, I still find a good deal of what I experienced difficult to believe, especially Hell House. The activity in Hell House was like nothing I had ever experienced before. Oh, I experienced various paranormal phenomena many years before Hell House, but not on the same scale as this investigation. For instance, upon the death of my former mother-in-law, my now deceased husband, Michael, brought her television, radio, and large microwave to our house. He placed the TV and radio in one of the spare bedrooms upstairs and the microwave on the kitchen counter. Almost immediately, we started experiencing all three appliances turning on and off at different times throughout the day and night. The TV was old and didn't have a remote, and none of our other remotes would work on it. It couldn't have been affected by a neighbor's remote because we were out of range. Our house was situated two acres away from the house on the right of us, and there was no house to the left of us. We were also situated about half an acre away from the road. We were unable to debunk any of the appliances. The radio had an alarm, but it wasn't set.

Just like the television and microwave, the radio turned on and off at random times. We would be watching TV in the living room and hear the microwave come on and run for a few minutes before turning off with the chime of the *done signal*. I went downstairs one morning to find the microwave running and very hot. I couldn't turn it off, so I unplugged it. We ended up unplugging all of those appliances and never trying to use them again. Michael and I both saw her apparition in our house on several different occasions. I was concerned that the ghost of my dead mother-in-law was living in our house, but Michael seemed to be accepting of her presence and even amused. I didn't try to move her on because I felt she was there as a result of Michael's unresolved emotional conflict regarding their relationship, which would make it very difficult for me to cross her over.

The world of Spirit consists of pure thought. Spirits who think alike are immediately attracted to each other, while those who think differently are repelled by each other. This is known as the law of attraction, and it operates much the same way in our physical world. You've probably heard the expression *birds of a feather flock together. This* is true of both worlds. Because of the law of attraction, I am able to discern between good and evil spirits based on their vibration and how they make me feel. If I am repelled by the energy of an entity, then I know it's evil. If I feel comfortable with a spirit, then I know it's okay. My guides and angels also give me information about the true nature of the spirits I encounter, so that I am protected.

Because spirits communicate through thought, they know when you are thinking of them and will come to you if you ask. Your loved ones in spirit really are just a thought away. Mediums are very sensitive individuals who perceive spirit communication with ease, but you don't have to be a medium to communicate with a deceased loved one. You can learn to initiate communication with Spirit and perceive signs of its presence. There are many accounts of spirits who have made spontaneous contact with mourning loved ones they left behind. This type of interaction between the dead and the living is referred to as after-death communication phenomena (ADCP). Although most after-death communications, or ADCs, occur spontaneously without any effort on the part of the living, it is possible to initiate communication by taking certain steps. If you want to learn more about how to communicate with your loved ones in spirit, you'll want to look for my book *Just a Thought Away: Communicating With Loved Ones in Spirit.*

I never cease to be amazed by spirits. They are able to communicate in such a way as to get their message across clearly, succinctly, and meaningfully. I might not always understand a message that spirit is sending through me, but my clients usually do.

About The Author

I am a natural Psychic Medium, which means I was born being able to perceive psychic information and communicate with the souls of people who have passed away. I remember perceiving spirit entities as early as the age of four or five. I was seven years old when I saw my first aura. At the age of nine, spirits started coming to me for help in delivering their messages or for help in crossing them over. Some of the spirits who contacted me just wanted to tell me their story, which I believe they needed to do to purge their souls from guilt or shame. I think they were looking for some type of absolution and telling their story provided them with the catharsis they needed to cross over. Aside from my psychic and mediumistic abilities, I am not much different from the average individual. I am a wife, mother, grandmother, certified grief counselor, certified transpersonal hypnotherapist, and RN. I hold a Bachelors of Science in Nursing, a Master's in Business Administration, and another Master's in the Science of Accounting. I live with my husband, Joe, and two cats, Zoey and Cecilia in the USA.

OTHER BOOKS BY THE AUTHOR I

Over the years hospitals have been perceived as havens of hope, healing, and birth. They have also been perceived as prisons of pain, suffering, and death. Because of the large number of deaths that occur at hospitals each day, it should come as no surprise that hospitals are very haunted. The earthbound souls that haunt hospitals may become trapped because they are confused, have unfinished business, are afraid of what awaits them on the other side, or are hungry for physical life and looking for someone they can easily possess to fulfill their fleshy desires. Regardless of the reasons spirits become trapped, these wayward souls can be found in every corridor and room inside a hospital. Hospitals are very haunted and I should know because I am a psychic nurse! Join me on my adventures into the fascinating world of spirits and haunted hospitals. After reading *My*

Cover Design by Shirley Smolko

Adventures as a Psychic Nurse & Medium: Haunted Hospitals! you may find yourself too scared to enter another hospital.

OTHER BOOKS BY THE AUTHOR II

A Workbook for Initiating After Death Communication

Shirley Smolko, RN, BSN, MBA, MSA, CHt, GC-C

The Venetian Medium

Cover Design by Shirley Smolko

Kubler-Ross's "Five Stages" of grief model focuses on an individual's acceptance of separation and integration of loss through these stages in order to resolve grief. Freud's "Grief Work" theory postulates that grief is resolved by severing bonds with the deceased. While these models may work for some, the "Continuing Bonds" theory is often a better alternative. This bereavement model states that healing grief is an ongoing process, and it is normal and healthy to stay connected to deceased loved ones in redefined ways. After-death communication enables the bereaved to make this connection and has been proven to significantly help individuals cope with death. Many grief stricken individuals consult with mediums to initiate communication with their loved ones in Spirit, but what if you could communicate directly with them without the help of a medium.

You can because they are just a thought away, and in this workbook, *Just a Thought Away: Communicating With Loved Ones in Spirit*, I show you how! To be released in Spring of 2021.

www.ingramcontent.com/pod-product-compliance
Lightning Source LLC
Chambersburg PA
CBHW071341080526
44587CB00017B/2917